THE EUROPEAN EMPIRES

THE ILLUSTRATED
HISTORY OF THE WORLD

VOLUME 8

THE EUROPEAN
EMPIRES

J. M. ROBERTS

New York
Oxford University Press

The Illustrated History of the World

This edition first published in 1999 in the United States of America by
Oxford University Press, Inc.,
198 Madison Avenue, New York, N.Y. 10016
Oxford is a registered trademark of Oxford University Press

THE EUROPEAN EMPIRES
Copyright © Editorial Debate SA 1998
Text Copyright © J. M. Roberts 1976, 1980, 1983, 1987, 1988, 1992, 1998
Artwork and Diagram Copyright © Editorial Debate SA 1998
(for copyright of photographs and maps, see acknowledgments on page 192, which are
to be regarded as an extension of this copyright)

Art Direction by Duncan Baird Publishers
Produced by Duncan Baird Publishers, London, England,
and Editorial Debate, Madrid, Spain

Series ISBN 0-19-521529-X
Volume ISBN 0-19-521526-5

DBP staff:
Senior editor: Joanne Levêque
Assistant editors: Georgina Harris, Kirsty Seymour-Ure
Senior designer: Steven Painter
Assistant designer: Anita Schnable
Picture research: Julia Ruxton
Sales fulfilment: Ian Smalley
Map artwork: Russell Bell
Decorative borders: Lorraine Harrison

Editorial Debate staff:
Editors and picture researchers:
Isabel Belmonte Martínez, Feliciano Novoa Portela,
Ruth Betegón Díez, Dolores Redondo
Editorial coordination: Ana Lucía Vila

Typeset in Sabon 11/15 pt
Color reproduction by Trescan, Madrid, Spain
Printed in Singapore by Imago Limited

NOTE
The abbreviations CE and BCE are used throughout this book:
CE Common Era (the equivalent of AD)
BCE Before Common Era (the equivalent of BC)

10 9 8 7 6 5 4 3 2

CONTENTS

THE EUROPEAN EMPIRES

HISTORICAL SUCCESS sometimes encourages short-term perspectives and judgments. The bald fact that in so many ways Europe ran the world at the beginning of the twentieth century encouraged Europeans to overlook the recent nature of their hegemony, and the very brief time for which it had been in existence. Not many of them could guess, either, how precarious that success might prove. For the moment, none the less, the domination of the interests of a minority of the world's population over the vast majority seemed assured. Only a few of them saw that the spread of European ideas, institutions and technology must in the end weaken European hegemony, even if only in its political expressions. One reason why its ephemeral, brief nature (in the long run of history, though more widespread than the hegemony of Rome, it did not last as long) went unrecognized was the richness and multiplicity of the ways in which it was expressed and worked. European hegemony was always much more than political or military domination, important and visible though these were. In diversity, in fact, lay its strength and the explanation why it lasted as long as it did. Similarly, the explanation of its waning and passing has to be sought in facts much more diverse than simple changes in power. A cultural tradition often itself appearing self-questioning and divided, Europe's own huge intestinal wars, the drifting away of economic power to new centres, all played their part – and all were in some measure visible to astute observers even before the twentieth century began.

By the end of the 19th century, the British Empire was the largest European empire in the world, and India was the "jewel in the crown" of that empire. Lord Curzon (1859–1925), shown here with his wife taking the lead role in a royal durbar (formal assembly) to show the strength of the British Raj in 1903, was viceroy of India from 1898 until 1905. Like many European colonialists of his generation, Curzon was convinced that he knew what was best for India and held the Indian Congress Party and the mood of growing nationalism in utter contempt. By 1918, however, when the British government conceded the principle of self-rule to India, European empires around the globe were threatened by increasingly insistent demands for independence.

1 THE EUROPEAN WORLD HEGEMONY

French officials pose with local Algerian leaders in front of a police station in Boghari in French-ruled Algeria. When this picture was taken (c.1900), European influence over the rest of the world was at its height and vast expanses of Asia, Africa and Oceania were under direct European control.

By 1900 THE PEOPLES of Europe and European stocks overseas dominated the globe. They did so in many different ways, some explicit and some implicit, but the qualifications matter less than the general fact. For the most part, the world responded to European initiatives and marched increasingly to European tunes. It is easy to overlook the fact that this was a sign of a unique development in world history. For the first time, one civilization established itself as a leader right round the globe. One minor consequence is that the remainder of this book will be increasingly concerned with a single, global, history.

It is important not to think only of the direct formal rule of the majority of the world's land-surface by European states (some people would prefer the term "Western" but this is unnecessarily finicky – the Americas and Antipodes are dominated by culture of European origin, not of Asian or African – and is also liable to suggest too much, because of the use of that word recently in a narrow political sense). There is economic and cultural hegemony to be considered, and European ascendancy was often expressed in influence as well as in overt control. The important distinction is between European forces which are aggressive, shaping, manipulative, and indigenous cultures and peoples which are the objects of those forces, and not often able to resist them effectively. It was by no means always to the disadvantage of non-Europeans that this was so, but they tended almost always to be the underdogs, those who adapted to the Europeans' world. At times they did so willingly, when they succumbed to the attractive

Time chart (1818–1888)

		1839 The French complete their conquest of Algeria	1842 China is opened to the West		1868 The "Meiji Restoration" begins in Japan	1884–1885 A conference on Africa is held in Berlin
1800				1850		1900
	1818 India becomes a British dominion		1834 Slavery is abolished in the British colonies		1869 The Suez Canal is opened	1888 Slavery is abolished in Brazil

The British Empire (and Protected Territories) 1815–1914

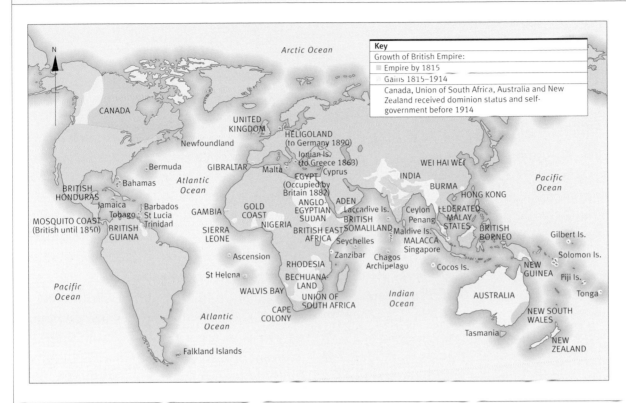

Key

Growth of British Empire:

Empire by 1815

Gains 1815–1914

Canada, Union of South Africa, Australia and New Zealand received dominion status and self-government before 1914

During the 19th century, the British expanded the territorial gains they had already made, mainly in Canada and India, to create the most important of the European colonial empires. At the height of the imperialist era, it was often remarked (as it had been earlier of the empire of Charles V) that the sun never set on the British Empire, so extensive was its reach.

force of Europe's progressive ideals or, most subtly of all, to new sets of expectations aroused by European teaching and example.

SPHERES OF EUROPEAN INFLUENCE

ONE WAY OF ENVISAGING the Europeans' world of 1900 is as a succession of concentric circles. The innermost was old Europe itself, which had grown in wealth and population for three centuries thanks to an increasing mastery first of its own and then of the world's resources. Europeans distinguished themselves more and more from other human beings by taking and consuming a growing share of the world's goods and by the energy and skill they showed in manipulating their environment. Their civilization was already rich in the nineteenth century

and was all the time getting richer. Industrialization had confirmed its self-feeding capacity to open up and create new resources; furthermore, the power generated by new wealth made possible the appropriation of the wealth of other parts of the world. The profits of Congo rubber, Burmese teak or Persian oil would not for a long time be reinvested in those countries. The poor European and American benefited from low prices for raw materials, and improving mortality rates tell the story of an industrial civilization finding it possible to give its peoples a richer life. Even the European peasant could buy cheap manufactured clothes and tools while his contemporaries in Africa and India still lived in the Stone Age.

This wealth was shared by the second circle of European hegemony, that of the European cultures transplanted overseas. The United States is the greatest example; Canada,

Australia, New Zealand, South Africa and the countries of South America make up the list. They did not all stand on the same footing towards the Old World, but together with Europe proper they were what is sometimes called the "Western world", an unhelpful expression, since they are scattered all round the globe, but one which seeks to express the important fact of the similarity of the ideas and institutions from which they were sprung. Of course, these were not all that had shaped them. They all had their distinctive frontiers, they all had faced special environmental challenges and unique historical circumstances. But what they had in common were ways of dealing with these challenges, institutions which different frontiers would reshape in different ways. They were all formally Christian – no one ever settled new lands in the name of atheism until the twentieth century – all regulated their affairs by European systems of law, and all had access to the great cultures of Europe with which they shared their languages.

THE IMPOSITION OF EUROPEAN VALUES

In 1900 the Europeanized world was sometimes called the "civilized world". It was called that just because it was a world of shared standards; the confident people who used the phrase could not easily see that there was much else deserving of the name of civilization in the world. When they looked for it, they tended to see only heathen, backward, benighted people or a few striving to join the civilized. Such an attitude was an important part of the story of European success; what were taken to be demonstrations of the inherent superiority of European ideas and values nerved individuals to fresh assaults on the world and inspired fresh incomprehension of it. The progressive values of the eighteenth century provided new arguments for superiority to reinforce those originally stemming from religion. By 1800, Europeans had lost almost all of their former respect for other civilizations. Their own social practice

The kingdom of Tonga in the Pacific Ocean was a British protectorate from 1900 until 1970. This photograph, which dates from c.1900, shows a British missionary in Tonga standing outside the Catholic Mission, accompanied by a group of local girls in European-style dress.

By 1830, most Latin American states had banned the slave trade, although slavery itself continued for several more decades. The abolition of slavery in Argentina by Juan Manuel de Rosas, dictator from 1835 to 1852, is commemorated in this 19th-century painting.

seemed obviously superior to the unintelligible barbarities found elsewhere. The advocacy of individual rights, a free press, universal suffrage, the protection of women, children (and even animals) from exploitation, have been ideals pursued right down to our own day in other lands by Europeans and Americans, often wholly unconscious that they might be inappropriate. Philanthropists and progressives long continued to be confident that the values of European civilization should be universalized as were its medicine and sanitation, even when deploring other assertions of European superiority. Science, too, has often appeared to point in the same direction, to the destruction of superstition and the bringing of the blessings of a rational exploitation of resources, the provision of formal education and the suppression of backward social customs. During the colonial era there was a well-nigh universal assumption that the values of European civilization were better than indigenous ones (obviously, too, they often were) and a large obliviousness to any disruptive effects they might have.

SUBJECT PEOPLES

Fortunately, it was thought, for the peoples of some of the lands over which "thick darkness" (as the Victorian hymn put it) brooded, they were by 1900 often ruled directly by Europeans or European stocks: subject peoples formed the third concentric circle of European civilization. In many colonies enlightened administrators toiled to bring the blessings of railways, Western education, hospitals, law and order to peoples whose own institutions had clearly failed (it was taken as evidence of their inadequacy that they had failed to stand up to the challenge and competition of a superior civilization). Even when native institutions were protected and preserved, it was from a position which assumed the superiority of the culture of the colonial power.

COLONIALISTS ABOLISH SLAVERY

Such conscious superiority is no longer admired or admissible. In one respect, it achieved an end, nevertheless, which the most scrupulous critics of colonialism still accept as a good one, even when suspecting the motives behind it. This was the abolition of slavery in the European world and the deployment of force and diplomacy to combat it even in countries Europeans did not control. The crucial steps were taken in 1807 and 1834, when the British parliament abolished first the trade in slaves and then slavery itself within the British Empire. This action by the major naval, imperial and commercial power was decisive; similar measures were soon enforced by other European nations, and slavery finished in the United States in 1865. The end of the process may be reckoned to be the emancipation of slaves in Brazil in 1888, at which date colonial governments and the Royal Navy were pressing hard on the operations of Arab slave-traders in the African continent and the Indian Ocean. Many forces, intellectual, religious, economic and political, went into this great achievement, and debate about their precise individual significance continues. It is perhaps worth pointing out here that though it was only after three

hundred years and more of large-scale slave-trading that abolition came, Europe's is also the only civilization which has ever eradicated slavery for itself. Though in the present century slavery briefly returned to Europe, it could not be sustained except by force, nor was it avowable as slavery. It cannot have been much consolation to their unhappy occupants, but the forced-labour camps of our own century were run by men who had to pay the tribute of hypocrisy to virtue by disguising their slaves as the subjects of re-education or judicial punishment.

BEYOND THE EUROPEAN SPHERE

BEYOND THIS OUTERMOST CIRCLE of directly ruled territories lay the rest of the world. Its peoples were shaped by Europe, too. Sometimes their values and institutions were corroded by contact with it – as was the case in the Chinese and Ottoman empires – and this might lead to indirect European political interference as well as the weakening of

The Meiji emperor Mitsuhito and his wife are depicted at the opening of the 1904 industrial fair in Tokyo. During Mitsuhito's reign (1868–1912), Japan's economy was transformed by the adoption of new ideas and technology from the West.

traditional authority. Sometimes they were stimulated by such contacts and exploited them: Japan is the only example of an important nation doing this with success. What was virtually impossible was to remain untouched by Europe. The busy, bustling energy of the European trader would alone have seen to that. In fact, it is the areas which were not directly ruled by Europeans which make the point of European supremacy most forcibly of all. European values were transferred on the powerful wings of aspiration and envy. Geographical remoteness was almost the only security (but even Tibet was invaded by the British in 1904). Ethiopia is virtually the solitary example of successful independence; it survived British and Italian invasion in the nineteenth century, but, of course, had the important moral advantage of claiming to have been a Christian country, albeit not a Western one and only intermittently, for some fourteen centuries.

MISSIONARY ACTIVITY

Whoever opened the door, a whole civilization was likely to try to follow them through it, but one of the most important agencies bringing European civilization to the rest of the world had always been Christianity, because of its virtually limitless interest in all sides of human behaviour. The territorial spread of the organized churches and the growth in their numbers of official adherents in the nineteenth century made this the greatest age of Christian expansion since apostolic times. Much of this was the result of a renewed wave of missionary activity; new orders were set up by Catholics, new societies for the support of overseas missions appeared in Protestant countries. Yet the paradoxical effect was the intensifying of the European flavour of what was supposedly a creed "for

all sorts and conditions of men," as the *English Book of Common Prayer* puts it. This is why Christianity was long seen as just one more aspect of European civilization, rather than as a spiritual message. Another interesting if trivial example was the concern missionaries often showed over dress. Whereas the Jesuits in seventeenth-century China had discreetly adopted the costume of their hosts, their nineteenth-century successors set to work with zeal to put Bantus and Solomon Islanders into European garments which were often of almost freakish unsuitability. This was one way in which Christian missionaries diffused more than a religious message. Often, too, they brought important material and technical benefits: food in time of famine, agricultural techniques, hospitals and schools, some of which could be disruptive of the societies which received them. Through them filtered the assumptions of a progressive civilization.

MILITARY SUPERIORITY

The ideological confidence of Europeans, missionaries and non-missionaries alike, could rest in the last resort on the knowledge

This engraving, which dates from 1882, depicts the African port of Lagos. Although the port was frequented by large numbers of European ships, the surrounding area appears to have been untouched by westernization, even in the late 19th century. Lagos is now the capital of Nigeria and one of the largest cities in Africa.

The colonial armies were mainly made up of native soldiers led by European commanding officers, as shown in this engraving of a French African frontier post in 1891.

that they could not be kept away even from countries which were not colonized. There appeared to be no part of the world where Europeans could not, if they wished, impose themselves by armed strength. The development of weapons in the nineteenth century gave Europeans an even greater relative advantage than they had enjoyed when the first Portuguese broadside was fired at Calicut. Even when advanced devices were available to other peoples, they could rarely deploy them effectively. At the battle of Omdurman in the Sudan in 1898 a British regiment opened fire on its opponents at 2,000 yards' range with the ordinary magazine rifle of the British army of the day. Soon afterwards, shrapnel shell and machine-guns were shredding to pieces the masses of the Mahdist army, who never reached the British line. By the end of the battle 10,000 of them had been killed for a loss of 48 British

and Egyptian soldiers. It was not, as an Englishman put it soon afterwards, simply the case that

Whatever happens, we have got
The Maxim gun, and they have not

for the Khalifa had machine-guns in his armoury at Omdurman, too. He also had telegraph apparatus to communicate with his forces and electric mines to blow up the British gunboats on the Nile. But none of these things was properly employed; not only a technical, but a mental transformation was required before non-European cultures could turn the instrumentation of the Europeans against them.

There was also one other sense, more benevolent and less disagreeable, in which European civilization rested upon force. This was because of the *Pax Britannica* which throughout the whole nineteenth century stood in the way of European nations fighting each other for mastery of the non-European world. There was no repeat performance of the colonial wars of the seventeenth and eighteenth centuries in the nineteenth, though the greatest extension of direct colonial rule in modern times was then going on. Traders of all nations could move without let or hindrance on the surface of the seas. British naval supremacy was a precondition of the informal expansion of European civilization.

A WORLD ECONOMY

BRITISH NAVAL STRENGTH guaranteed, above all, the international framework of trade whose centre, by 1900, was Europe. The old peripheral exchanges by a few merchants and enterprising captains had, from the seventeenth century onwards, been replaced gradually by integrated relationships of inter-

Military superiority was crucial to the European empires' rapid expansion. This engraving depicts Anglo-Egyptian troops entering the Sudanese city of Omdurman in 1898. Led by Commander-in-Chief Kitchener, they had easily defeated the Mahdist army.

dependence based on a broad distinction of role between industrial and non-industrial countries; the second tended to be primary producers meeting the needs of the increasingly urbanized populations of the first. But this crude distinction needs much qualification. Individual countries often do not fit it; the United States, for example, was both a great primary producer and the world's leading manufacturing power in 1914, with an output as great as those of Great Britain, France and Germany together. Nor was this distinction one which ran exactly between nations of European and non-European culture. Japan and Russia were both industrializing faster than China or India in 1914, but Russia, though European, Christian and imperialist, could certainly not be regarded as a developed nation, and most Japanese (like most Russians) were still peasants. Nor could a developed economy be found in Balkan Europe. All that can be asserted is that in 1914 a nucleus of advanced countries existed with social and economic structures quite different from those of traditional society, and that these were the core of an Atlantic group of nations which was increasingly the world's main producer and consumer.

THE PIVOTAL ROLE OF GREAT BRITAIN

The world economy came to a sharp focus in London, where the financial services which sustained the flow of world trade were centred. A huge amount of the world's business was transacted by means of the sterling bill of exchange; it rested in turn upon the international gold standard which sustained confidence by ensuring that the main currencies remained in fairly steady relationships with one another. All major countries had gold currencies and travel anywhere in the world was possible with a bag of gold sovereigns, five-dollar pieces, gold francs or any other major medium of exchange without any doubts about their acceptability.

London was also in another sense the centre of the world economy because although the United Kingdom's gross output was by 1914 overtaken in important respects by that of the United States and Germany, she

Attempting to fight the Europeans meant acquiring their weapons. This engraving, dated 1884, shows Sudanese Mahdist soldiers carrying European guns. Without the Western armies' tactics and discipline, however, such weapons brought only brief success.

The Royal Exchange building, seen in this late 19th-century image, was at the heart of the London Stock Exchange.

was the greatest of trading nations. The bulk of the world's shipping and carrying trade was in British hands. She was the main importing and exporting nation and the only one which sent more of its manufactures to non-European nations than to European. Great Britain was also the biggest exporter of capital and drew a huge income from her overseas investments, notably those in the United States and South America. Her special role imposed a roughly triangular system of international exchange. The British bought goods, manufactured and otherwise, from Europe and paid for them with their own manufactures, cash and overseas produce. To the rest of the world they exported manufactures, capital and services, taking in return food and raw materials and cash. This complex system illustrates how little the European relationship with the rest of the world was a simple one of exchanging manufactures for raw materials. And there was, of course, always the unique instance of the United States, little involved in export, but gradually

commanding a greater and greater share of its own domestic market for manufactured goods, and still a capital importer.

FREE TRADE

Most British economists believed in 1914 that the prosperity which this system enjoyed and the increasing wealth which it made possible showed the truth of free trade doctrine. Their own country's prosperity had grown most rapidly in the heyday of such ideas. Adam Smith had predicted that prosperity would continue if a closed imperial system reserving trade to the mother country were abandoned and so, in the case of America, it had soon proved, for a big expansion had come to the Anglo-American trade within a few years of the peace of 1783. By 1800 a majority of British exports were already going outside Europe and there then still lay ahead the greatest period of expansion of trade in India and East Asia. Understandably, British imperial policy was directed not to the potentially embarrassing acquisition of new colonies, but to the opening of areas closed to trade, for that was where prosperity was deemed to lie. One outstanding example was the Opium War of 1839–42. The outcome was the opening of five Chinese ports to European trade and the de facto cession to Great Britain of Hong Kong as a base for the exercise of a jurisdiction inseparable from the management of commerce.

In the middle of the nineteenth century there had been for a couple of decades a high tide of free trade ideas when more governments seemed willing to act upon them than ever before or after. In this phase, tariff barriers were demolished and the comparative advantage of the British, first among trading and manufacturing nations, had continued. But this era passed in the 1870s and

This photograph was taken c.1900 in an opium den in China. Although the opium trade had been banned in 1800, it has been estimated that there may have been as many as 10 million Chinese addicts by 1830. The mainly British merchants who imported the drug to China from India, where it was produced, could earn enormous profits.

1880s. The onset of a worldwide recession of economic activity and falling prices meant that by 1900 Great Britain was again the only major nation without tariffs for protection and even in that country questioning of the old free trade dogmas was beginning to be heard as competition from Germany grew fiercer and more alarming.

ECONOMIC INTEGRATION

By comparison with that of today the economic world of 1914 seems to be one of astonishing economic freedom and confidence. A long European peace provided the soil in which trading connexions could mature. Stable currencies assured great flexibility to a world price system; exchange control existed nowhere in the world and Russia and China were by then as completely integrated into this market as other countries. Freight and insurance rates had grown

This painting, entitled *Oil Creek Valley in 1871*, depicts rigs for extracting crude oil in Pennsylvania in the United States. The first oil well had been sunk in Pennsylvania in 1857 and it was the first region in the world to boast a large-scale operation to extract oil.

cheaper and cheaper, food prices had shown a long-term decline and wages had shown a long-term rise. Interest rates and taxation were low. It seemed as if a capitalist paradise might be achievable.

As this system had grown to incorporate Asia and Africa, it, too, came to be instrumental in a diffusion of ideas and techniques originally European, but soon acclimatized in other lands. Joint stock companies, banks, commodity and stock exchanges spread round the world by intrusion and imitation; they began to displace traditional structures of commerce. The building of docks and railways, the infrastructures of world trade, together with the beginnings of industrial employment, began in some places to turn peasants into an industrial proletariat. Sometimes the effects on local economies could be bad; the cultivation of indigo in

India, for example, more or less collapsed when synthetic dyes became available in Germany and Great Britain. Isolation first disturbed by explorers, missionaries and soldiers was destroyed by the arrival of the telegraph and the railway; in the twentieth century the motor car would take this further. Deeper relationships were being transformed, too; the canal opened at Suez in 1869 not only shaped British commerce and strategy, but gave the Mediterranean new importance, not this time as a centre of a special civilization, but as a route.

THE CULTURAL IMBALANCE

Economic integration and institutional change were inseparable from cultural contamination. The formal instruments of

The British built an extensive railway network in India from the mid-19th century. This early 20th-century photograph shows the entrance to the Barogh Tunnel on the Kalka–Simla Railway, north of Delhi. The narrow-gauge railway, which was completed in 1903, connected the town of Kalka with the hill station of Simla, where the British government of India convened every summer from 1865 until 1939.

The Suez Canal

In the 7th century BCE the Egyptian king Necho II was the first ruler to try, in vain, to link the Red Sea to the Mediterranean. In 522 BCE, the Persian king Darius I restored and completed the canal, thus creating a crucial direct maritime link between Egypt and Persia. Although the canal was improved during Roman times, little by little it silted up until it became unnavigable and it was abandoned.

In 1854, the French diplomat Ferdinand de Lesseps was granted permission by Muhammad Said Pasha, the viceroy of the Ottoman Empire, to start work on a canal that would link Suez directly to the Mediterranean. With financial support from French shareholders, work began in 1859, despite attempts by the British government to prevent the project from going ahead. Although prisoners were initially used to carry out the construction work, they were eventually replaced by mechanical excavators; some 3 million cubic metres (3.9 million cubic yards) of sand were dug out in total. A fresh-water canal had to be built to supply the 25,000 workers with drinking water and a new city, named Port Said, was established at the Mediterranean end of the canal.

In November 1869 the Suez Canal was finally completed. The opening ceremony was attended by 6,000 guests, including the French empress Eugénie and other figureheads of European royalty. The finished canal was 105 miles (169 km) long, 190 ft (58 m) wide at the surface and 72 ft (22 m) wide at the bottom, and had an average depth of 26 ft (8 m). It allowed maritime traffic to travel between the Red Sea and the Mediterranean, thus cutting the distance between European and Asian ports by more than 4,350 miles (7,000 km).

In 1875, Great Britain acquired the majority of the shares of the company, which it kept until Nasser, the Egyptian president, nationalized the canal in 1956. More recently, during the Six Day War between Egypt and Israel in 1967, the canal was blocked by sunken ships, and it remained closed until 1975.

The first ships sail through the Suez Canal on its opening day, 17 November, 1869. Because it drastically reduced the sailing time between Europe and Asia, the canal became an essential route for Europe's commercial expansion and a vital axis of the British Empire.

Members of the Japanese army are pictured c.1875, with their German military advisers. The Japanese soldiers are dressed in European-style uniforms that are modelled on those of the Germans. Many Japanese saw the adoption of European dress as a sign of progress.

missionary religion, educational institutions and government policy are only a tiny part of this story. The European languages which were used officially, for example, took with them European concepts and opened to educated élites in non-European countries the heritage not only of Christian civilization, but of secular and "enlightened" European culture, too. Missionaries spread more than dogma or medical and educational services; they also provoked the criticism of the colonial régime itself, because of the gap between its performance and the pretensions of the culture it imposed.

In the perspectives of the twentieth century, much of what is most durable and important in the impact of Europe on the world can be traced to such unintended, ambiguous effects as these. Above all, there was the simple urge to imitate, whether expressed ludicrously in the adoption of European dress or, much more importantly, in the conclusion drawn by many who sought to

resist European hegemony that to do so it was necessary to adopt European ways. Almost everywhere, radicals and reformers advocated Europeanization. The ideas of 1776, 1789 and 1848 are still at work in Asia and Africa and the world still debates its future in European terms.

This extraordinary outcome is too often overlooked. In its unravelling, 1900 is only a vantage point, not the end of the story. The Japanese are a gifted people who have inherited exquisite artistic traditions, yet they have adopted not only Western industrialism (which is understandable enough) but Western art forms, Western dress and even Western drink in preference to their own. Though the Japanese find whisky and claret fashionable, saké has not yet swept Europe or the United States. The Chinese officially revere Marx, a German philosopher who articulated a system of thought rooted in nineteenth-century German idealism and English social and economic facts, who rarely spoke of Asia except with contempt and never went east of Prussia in his life. This suggests another curious fact: the balance-sheet of cultural influence is overwhelmingly one-sided. The world gave back to Europe occasional fashions, but no idea or institution of comparable effect to those Europe gave to the world. The teaching of Marx was long a force throughout twentieth-century Asia; the last non-European whose words had any comparable authority in Europe was Jesus Christ.

THE GREAT RESETTLEMENT

ONE PHYSICAL TRANSMISSION of culture was achieved by the movement of Europeans to other continents. Outside the United States, the two most numerous groups of European communities overseas were (as they still are) in South America and the former British colonies of white settlement which, though formally subject to London's direct rule for much of the nineteenth century, were in fact long oddly hybrid, not quite independent nations, but not really colonies either. Both groups were fed during the nineteenth century, like the United States, by the great diaspora of Europeans whose numbers justify one name which has been given to this era of European demography: the Great Resettlement. Before 1800, there was little European emigration except from the British Isles. After that date, something like sixty million Europeans went overseas, and this tide began to flow strongly in the 1830s. In the nineteenth century most of it went to North America, and then to Latin America (especially Argentina and Brazil), to Australia and South Africa. At the same time a concealed

At the end of the 19th century, emigration to America seemed, to many Europeans, to offer opportunities that did not exist in the Old World. This engraving from 1878 shows emigrants in Hamburg, Germany, boarding a transatlantic liner bound for the United States.

European emigration was also occurring across land within the Russian empire, which occupied one-sixth of the world's land surface and which had vast spaces to draw migrants in Siberia. The peak of European emigration overseas actually came on the eve of the First World War, in 1913, when over a million and a half left Europe; over a third of these were Italians, nearly four hundred thousand were British and two hundred thousand Spanish. Fifty years earlier, Italians figured only to a minor degree, Germans and Scandinavians loomed much larger. All the time, the British Isles contributed a steady flow; between 1880 and 1910 eight and a half million Britons went overseas (the Italian figure for this period was just over six million).

The greatest number of British emigrants went to the United States (about 65 per cent of them between 1815 and 1900), but large numbers went also to the self-governing colonies; this ratio changed after 1900 and by 1914 a majority of British emigrants was going to the latter. Italians and Spaniards also went to South America in large numbers, though Italians preferred the United States. That country remained the greatest of the receivers for all other nationalities; between 1820 and 1950 the United States benefited by the arrival of over thirty-three million Europeans.

REASONS FOR EUROPEAN AND ASIAN MIGRATION

Explanations of the striking demographic evolution caused by migration are not far to seek. Politics sometimes contributed to the flow, as it did after 1848. Rising populations in Europe always pressed upon economic possibilities as the discovery of the phenomenon of "unemployment" shows. In the last decades of the nineteenth century, too, when emigration was rising fastest, European farmers were pressed by overseas competition. Above all, it mattered that for the first time in human history there were obvious opportunities in other lands, where labour was needed, at a moment when there were suddenly easier and cheaper means of getting there. The steamship and railroad greatly changed demographic history and they both began to produce their greatest effect after 1880. They permitted much greater local mobility, so that temporary migrations of labour and movements within continents became much easier. Great Britain exported Irish peasants, Welsh miners and steelworkers and English farmers; she took in at the end of the nineteenth century an influx of Jewish communities from Eastern Europe which remained a distinguishable element in British society. To the seasonal migration of labour which had always characterized such border districts as southern France were now added longer-term movements as Poles came to France to work in

The large numbers of immigrants arriving in the United States during the second half of the 19th century produced xenophobic reactions. In this cartoon, dated 1888, a mixed group of immigrants gawps at the "last genuine Yankee" in a street where foreign shops advertise themselves as American. In spite of prejudice, the integration of people of diverse origins into the American culture was broadly successful.

coal-mines and Italian waiters and ice-cream men became part of British folklore. When political changes made the North African shore accessible, it, too, was changed by short-range migration from Europe; Italians, Spanish and French were drawn there to settle or trade in the coastal cities and created a new society with interests distinct both from those of the societies from which the migrants had come and from those of the native societies beside which they had settled.

Easier travel did not only ease European migration. Chinese and Japanese settlement on the Pacific coasts of North America was already important by 1900. Chinese migrants also moved down into Southeast Asia, Japanese to Latin America; the spectacle frightened Australians, who sought to preserve a "White Australia" by limiting immigration by racial criteria. The British Empire provided a huge framework within which Indian communities spread round the world. But these movements, though important, were subordinate to the major phenomenon of the nineteenth century, the last great *Völkerwanderung* of the European peoples, and one as decisive for the future as the barbarian invasions had been.

SPANISH AMERICA

In "LATIN AMERICA" (the term was invented in the middle of the nineteenth century), which attracted in the main Italians and Spaniards, southern Europeans could find much that was familiar. There was the framework to cultural and social life provided by Catholicism; there were Latin languages and social customs. The political and legal framework also reflected the imperial past, some of whose institutions had persisted through an era of political upheaval at the beginning of the nineteenth

century which virtually ended Spanish and Portuguese colonial rule on the mainland. This happened because events in Europe had led to a crisis in which weaknesses in the old empires proved fatal.

This was not for want of effort, at least on the part of the Spanish. In contrast to the British in the north, the metropolitan government had carried out sweeping reforms in the eighteenth century. When the Bourbons replaced the last Habsburg on the Spanish throne in 1701 a new era of Spanish imperial development had begun, though it took some decades to become apparent. When changes came they led first to reorganization and then to "enlightened" reform. The two viceroyalties of 1700 became four, two more appearing in New Granada (Panama and the area covered by Ecuador, Colombia and Venezuela), and La Plata, which ran from the mouth of the river across the continent to the border of Peru. This structural rationalization was followed by relaxations of the closed commercial system, at first unwillingly conceded and then consciously promoted as a means to prosperity. These stimulated the

For poor 19th-century emigrants, such as these Irish families, the long journey to America was often undertaken in dire conditions.

economy both of the colonies and of those parts of Spain (notably the Mediterranean littoral) which benefited from the ending of the monopoly of colonial trade hitherto confined to the port of Seville.

None the less, these healthy tendencies were offset by grave weaknesses which they did not touch. A series of insurrections revealed deep-seated ills. In Paraguay (1721–35), Colombia (1781) and, above all, Peru (1780) there were real threats to colonial government which could only be contained by great military efforts. Among others, these required levies of colonial militia, a double-edged expedient, for it provided the Creoles with military training which they might turn against Spain. The deepest division in Spanish colonial society was between the Indians and the colonists of Spanish descent, but that between the Creoles and *peninsulares* was to have more immediate political importance. It had widened with the passage of time. Resentful of their exclusion from high office, the Creoles noted the success of the British colonists of North America in shaking off imperial rule. The French Revolution, too, at first suggested possibilities rather than dangers.

This watercolour celebrates the proclamation of Agustín de Iturbide as emperor of the newly independent Mexico (1822). Two years later, Iturbide was dethroned by a republican uprising. For a long time, life in the new Latin American states was characterized by political instability and civil conflict.

THE WARS OF INDEPENDENCE

As insurrections threatened the colonies, the Spanish government was embarrassed in other ways. In 1790 a quarrel with Great Britain led at last to surrender of the remnants of the old Spanish claim to sovereignty throughout the Americas, when it conceded that the right to prohibit trade or settlement in North America only extended within an area of thirty miles around a Spanish settlement. Then came wars, first with France, then with Great Britain (twice), and finally with France again, during the Napoleonic invasion. These wars not only cost Spain Santo Domingo, Trinidad and Louisiana, but also its dynasty, which was forced by Napoleon to abdicate in 1808. The end of Spanish sea-power had already come at Trafalgar. In this state of disorder and weakness, when, finally, Spain itself was engulfed by French invasion, the Creoles decided to break loose and in 1810 the Wars of Independence began with risings in New Granada, La Plata and New Spain. The Creoles were not at first successful and in Mexico they found that they had a racial war on their hands when the Indians took the opportunity to turn on all whites. But the Spanish government was not able to win them over nor to muster sufficient strength to crush further waves of rebellion. British sea-power guaranteed that no conservative European power could step in to help the Spanish and thus practically sustained the Monroe doctrine. So, there emerged from the fragments of the former Spanish Empire a collection of republics, most of them ruled by soldiers.

In Portuguese Brazil the story had gone differently, for though a French invasion of Portugal had in 1807 provoked a new departure, it was different from that of the Spanish empire. The prince regent of Portugal had himself removed from Lisbon to Rio de

S lave labour played an important role in the economy of colonial Brazil. In this 18th-century engraving, slaves working in a diamond mine are watched by white foremen brandishing whips.

Janeiro which thus became the effective capital of the Portuguese Empire. Though he went back to Portugal as king in 1820 he left behind his son, who took the lead in resisting an attempt by the Portuguese government to reassert its control of Brazil and, with relatively little fighting, became the emperor of an independent Brazil in 1822.

Post-colonial South America

EL SALVADOR 1838
NICARAGUA 1838
(Mosquito Coast to Nicaragua 1860)
Caribbean Sea
HONDURAS 1838
Panama
VENEZUELA 1830
Caracas
BRITISH
Georgetown
DUTCH
Paramaribo
FRENCH
Cayenne
GUIANA
Atlantic Ocean
PANAMA 1903
COSTA RICA 1838
Bogotá
COLOMBIA 1831
(name taken in 1861)
Quito
ECUADOR 1830
Amazon
BRAZIL 1822
(empire until 1889)
Lima
PERU 1821
Brasilia
La Paz
BOLIVIA 1825
Pacific Ocean
PARAGUAY 1811
Asunción
Rio de Janeiro
São Paulo
ARGENTINA 1810
(Argentine Confederation until 1853)
URUGUAY 1828
N
Santiago
Buenos Aires
Montevideo
Plate
CHILE 1818
Atlantic Ocean
Falkland Islands (to UK 1833)

Key
- Main block of territory disputed and changing hands during the wars of the 19th century
- European possessions
- All dates refer to year of independence

0   1,600 km
0   1,000 miles

SOUTH AMERICA AFTER INDEPENDENCE

Between 1810 and 1822, the whole of South America, except for the Guyanas, proclaimed its independence. The new borders, which were often drawn through regions that were almost totally uninhabited, took time to become established and gave rise to several conflicts. In the 19th century, the most important of these were the Triple Alliance War (1864–1870) in which Argentina, Brazil and Uruguay defeated Paraguay, and the Pacific War (1878–1883), in which Chile defeated Peru and Bolivia.

A glance at the map of contemporary South America reveals the most obvious of many great differences between the revolution of 1776 and those of 1810 onwards: no United States of South America emerged from the Wars of Independence. Although the great hero and leader of independence, Bolívar, hoped for much from a Congress of the new states at Panama in 1826, nothing came of it.

It is not difficult to understand why. For all the variety of the thirteen British colonies and difficulties facing them, they had after their victory relatively easy intercommunication by sea and few insurmountable obstacles of terrain. They also had some experience of co-operation and a measure of direction of their own affairs even while under imperial rule. With these advantages, their divisions still remained important enough to impose a constitution which gave very limited powers to the national government. It is hardly surprising that the southern republics could not achieve continental unity for all the advantages of the common background of Spanish rule which most of them shared.

The absence of unifying factors may not have been disadvantageous, for the Latin Americans of the early nineteenth century faced no danger or opportunity which made unity desirable. Against the outside world they were protected by Great Britain and the United States. At home the problems of post-colonial evolution were far greater than had been anticipated and were unlikely to be tackled more successfully by the creation of an artificial unity. Indeed, as in Africa a century and a half later, the removal of colonial rule revealed that geography and community did not always suit political units which corresponded to the old administrative divisions. The huge, thinly populated states which emerged from the Wars of Independence were constantly in danger of falling apart into small units as the urban minorities who had guided the independence movement found it impossible to control their followers. Some did break up. There were racial problems, too; the social inequalities they gave rise to were not removed by independence. Not every country experienced them in the same way. In Argentina, for example, the relatively small Indian population underwent near-extermination at the hands of the army. That

country was celebrated by the end of the nineteenth century for the extent to which it resembled Europe in the domination of European strains in its population. At the other extreme, Brazil had a population the majority of which was black and, at the time of independence, much of it still in slavery. Intermarriage was not frowned upon, and the result is a population which may well be the most successfully integrated ethnic mix in the world today.

POLITICAL DIFFICULTIES

The new Latin American states could not draw upon any tradition of self-government

Benito Juárez, a Mexican of indigenous Indian blood, was one of the instigators of Mexico's progressive constitution of 1857 and was elected president in 1861. Juárez fought against the French invasion, which temporarily made Maximilian of Austria emperor of Mexico. After defeating Maximilian in 1870, Juárez once again took the office of president, which he held until his death in 1872.

Military force has often decided Latin American political struggles. This scene from the brief civil war that took place in Chile in 1891 shows the navy attacking the port of Valparaiso in support of a conservative congress against the reformist president José Manuel Balmaceda.

the long run inevitable, given its huge power as a landowner and popular influence, but unfortunate in adding anti-clericalism to the woes of the continent. In these circumstances, it was hardly surprising that during most of the century each republic found that its affairs tended to drift into the hands of *caudillos*, military adventurers and their cliques who controlled armed forces sufficient to give them sway until more powerful rivals came along.

The cross-currents of civil war and wars between the new states – some very bloody – led by 1900 to a map which is still much the same today. Mexico, the most northern of the former Spanish colonies, had lost land in the north to the United States. Four mainland Central American republics had appeared and two island states, the Dominican Republic and Haiti. Cuba was on the point of achieving independence. To the south were the ten states of South America. All of these countries were republican; Brazil had given up its monarchy in 1889. Though all had been through grave civic disorders, they represented very different degrees of stability and constitutional propriety. In Mexico, an Indian had indeed become president, to great effect, in the 1860s, but everywhere there remained the social divisions between Indians and the *mestizos* (those of mixed blood) on the one hand, and those of European blood (much reinforced in numbers when immigration became more rapid after 1870) on the other. The Latin American countries had contained about 19 million people in 1800; a century later they had 63 million.

in facing their many problems, for the colonial administrations had been absolutist and had not thrown up representative institutions. For the political principles they sought to apply, the leaders of the republics looked in the main to the French Revolution, but these were advanced ideas for states whose tiny élites did not even share among themselves agreement about accepted practice; they could hardly produce a framework of mutual tolerance. Worse still, revolutionary principles quickly brought the Church into politics, a development which was perhaps in

LATIN AMERICAN WEALTH

Large-scale immigration argues a certain increase in wealth. Most of the Latin American countries had important natural resources in one form or another. Sometimes, they fought over them for such advantages became even more valuable as Europe and the United States became more industrialized. Argentina had space and some of the finest pasture in the world: the invention of refrigerator ships in the 1880s made her England's butcher and later grain grower as well. At the end of the nineteenth century, she was the richest of the Latin American countries. Chile had nitrates (taken from Bolivia and Peru in the "War of the Pacific" of 1879–83) and Venezuela had oil; both grew more important with the twentieth century. Mexico had oil, too. Brazil had practically everything except oil, above all coffee and sugar. The list could be continued but would confirm that the growing wealth of Latin America came above all from primary produce. The capital to exploit this came from Europe and the United States and this produced new ties between these European nations overseas and Europe itself.

This increase in wealth nevertheless was connected with two related drawbacks. One was that it did little to reduce the disparities of wealth to be found in these countries;

indeed, they may have increased. In consequence, social, like racial, tensions remained largely unresolved. An apparently Europeanized urban élite lived lives wholly unlike those of the Indian and *mestizo* masses. This was accentuated by the dependence of Latin America on foreign capital. Not unreasonably, foreign investors sought security. They by no means always got it, but it tended to lead them to support of the existing social

A street in Rio de Janeiro in 1827 is portrayed in this contemporary scene. The slaves' elegant livery was an external sign of the great wealth of the city's élite Europeanized families.

This engraving, which is dated 1854, depicts the Plaza de la Independencia in Santiago de Chile. The square is lined with imposing European-style buildings.

and political authorities, who thus enhanced still further their own wealth. It would take only a few years of the twentieth century for conditions resulting from this sort of thing to produce social revolution in Mexico.

RELATIONS WITH THE UNITED STATES

The irritation and disappointment of foreign investors who could not collect the debts due to them led sometimes to diplomatic conflicts and even armed intervention. The collection of debt was, after all, not seen as a revival of colonialism and European governments sent stiff messages and backed them up with force on several occasions during the century. When in 1902 Great Britain, Germany and Italy together instituted a naval blockade of Venezuela in order to collect debts due to their subjects who had suffered in revolutionary troubles, this provoked the United States to go further than the Monroe doctrine.

From the days of the Texan republic

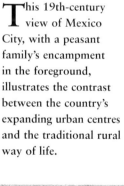

This 19th-century view of Mexico City, with a peasant family's encampment in the foreground, illustrates the contrast between the country's expanding urban centres and the traditional rural way of life.

onwards, the relations of the United States with its neighbours had never been easy: nor are they today. Too many complicating factors were at work. The Monroe doctrine expressed the basic interest of the United States in keeping the hemisphere uninvolved with Europe, and the first Pan-American Congress was another step in this direction when the United States organized it in 1889. But this could no more prevent the growth of economic links with Europe than could the Revolution sever those of the United States with Great Britain (and North Americans were among the investors in South American countries and soon had their special pleas to make to their government). Moreover, as the century came to an end, it was clear that the strategic situation which was the background to the Monroe doctrine had changed. Steamships and the rise of American interest in the Far East and the Pacific were the main causes of change. This made the United States much more sensitive, in particular, to developments in Central America and the Caribbean, where an isthmian canal was more and more likely to be built.

UNITED STATES INTERVENTION IN LATIN AMERICA

The outcome of the changing strategic situation was greater heavy-handedness and even arrogance in United States policy towards its neighbours in the early twentieth century. When, after a brief war with Spain, the United States won Cuba its independence (and took Puerto Rico from Spain for herself), special restraints were incorporated in the new Cuban constitution to ensure she would remain a satellite. The territory of the Panama Canal was obtained by intervention in the affairs of Colombia. The Venezuelan debt affair was followed by an even more remarkable assertion of American strength – a "corollary" to the Monroe doctrine. This was the announcement (almost at once given practical expression in Cuba and the Dominican Republic) that the United States would exercise a right of intervention in the affairs of any state in the western hemisphere whose internal affairs were in such disorder that they might tempt European intervention. Later, one American president sent marines to Nicaragua in 1912 on this ground and another occupied the Mexican port of Vera Cruz in 1914 as a way of coercing a Mexican government. In 1915 a protectorate was established by treaty over Haiti which was to last forty years.

This was not the end of an unhappy story of relations between the United States and her neighbours, though far enough to take it for the moment. Their importance here, in any case, is only symptomatic of the ambiguous standing of the Latin American states in rela tion to Europe. Rooted in its culture, tied to it by economics, they none the less were con strained politically to avoid entanglement with it. This did not, of course, mean that they did not stand, so far as Europeans were concerned, on the white man's side of the great distinction more and more drawn between those within the pale of European civilization and those outside it. When Europeans thought of "Latin Americans" they thought of those of European descent, the urban, literate, privileged minority, not the Indian and black masses.

BRITISH COLONIALISM

THE CRUMBLING of the Spanish Empire so soon after the defection of the thirteen colonies long led many people to expect that the other settler colonies of the British Empire would soon throw off the rule of London,

KITH AND KIN.

Canada (to Britannia). "IF I CAN BE OF ANY ASSISTANCE, COMMAND ME." (And so say Victoria and New South Wales.)

This cartoon, which appeared in the British magazine *Punch* on 21 February, 1885, shows a personification of the Dominion of Canada loyally offering to fight for Britannia.

too. In a way, this happened, but hardly as had been anticipated. At the end of the nineteenth century, the British magazine *Punch* printed a patriotic cartoon in which the British Lion looked approvingly at rows of little lion-cubs, armed and uniformed, who represented the colonies overseas. They were appropriately dressed as soldiers, for the volunteer contingents sent from other parts of the empire to fight for the British in the war they were then engaged upon in South Africa were of major importance. A century earlier, no one could have anticipated that a single colonial soldier would be available to the mother country. The year 1783 had burnt deep into the consciousness of British statesmen. Colonies, they thought they had learnt, were tricky things, costing money, conferring few benefits, engaging the metropolitan country in fruitless strife with other powers and native peoples and in the end usually turning round to bite the hand that fed them. The distrust of colonial entanglements which such views engendered helped to swing British imperial interest towards the East at the end

In Montreal, in the British Dominion of Canada, a train crosses the frozen Saint Lawrence River in 1880. Thick beams have been laid across the ice to support the sleepers – a remarkable technical feat for any age.

of the eighteenth century, towards the possibilities of Asian trade. It seemed that in the Far East there would be no complications caused by European settlers and in Eastern seas no need for expensive forces which could not easily be met by the Royal Navy.

SELF-GOVERNING DEPENDENCIES

Broadly speaking, wariness about potentially problematic colonies was to be the prevailing attitude in British official circles during the whole nineteenth century. It led them to tackle the complicated affairs of each colony in ways which sought, above all else, economy and the avoidance of trouble. In the huge spaces of Canada and Australia this led, stormily, to the eventual uniting of the individual colonies in federal structures with responsibility for their own government. In 1867 the Dominion of Canada came into existence, and in 1901 there followed the Commonwealth of Australia. In each case, union had been preceded by the granting of responsible government to the original colonies and in each case there had been special difficulties. In Canada the outstanding one was the existence of a French Canadian

community in the province of Quebec, in Australia the clashes of interest between settlers and convicts – of whom the last consignment was delivered in 1867. Each, too, was a huge, thinly populated country which could only gradually be pulled together to generate a sense of nationality. In each case the process was slow: it was not until 1885 that the last spike was driven on the transcontinental line of the Canadian Pacific Railway, and transcontinental railways in Australia were delayed for a long time by the adoption of different gauges in different states. In the end, nationalism was assisted by the growth of awareness of potential external threats – United States economic strength and Asian immigration – and, of course, by bickering with the British.

New Zealand also achieved responsible government, but one less decentralized, as befitted a much smaller country. Europeans had arrived there from the 1790s onwards and they found a native people, the Maori, with an advanced and complex culture, whom the visitors set about corrupting. Missionaries followed, and did their best to keep out settlers and traders. But they arrived just the same. When it seemed that a French entrepreneur was likely to establish a French interest, the British government at last reluctantly gave way to the pressure brought upon it by missionaries and some of the settlers and proclaimed British sovereignty in 1840. In 1856 the colony was given responsible government and only wars with the Maoris delayed the withdrawal of British soldiers until 1870. Soon afterwards, the old provinces lost their remaining legislative powers. In the later years of the century, New Zealand governments showed remarkable independence and vigour in the pursuit of advanced social welfare policies and achieved full self-government in 1907.

That was the year after a Colonial

Conference in London had decided that the name "Dominion" should in future be used for all the self-governing dependencies, which meant, in effect, the colonies of white settlement. One more remained to be given this status before 1914, the Union of South Africa, which came into existence in 1910. This was the end of a long and unhappy chapter – the unhappiest in the history of the British Empire and one which closed only to open another in the history of Africa which within a few decades looked even more bleak.

SOUTH AFRICA

No BRITISH COLONISTS had settled in South Africa until after 1814, when Great Britain for strategical reasons retained the former Dutch colony at the Cape of Good Hope. This was called "Cape Colony" and there soon arrived some thousands of British settlers who, though outnumbered by the Dutch, had the backing of the British government in introducing British assumptions and law. This opened a period of whittling away of the privileges of the Boers, as the Dutch farmers were called. In particular, they were excited and irked by any limitation of their freedom to deal with the native African as they wished. Their especial indignation was aroused when, as a result of the general abolition of slavery in British territory, some 35,000 of their black slaves were freed with, it was said, inadequate compensation. Convinced that the British would not abandon a policy favourable to the native African – and, given the pressures upon British governments, this was a reasonable view – a great exodus of Boers took place in 1835. This Great Trek north across the Orange River was of radical importance in

After defeating the Zulus in South Africa, the British authorities came to an agreement with them. The Zulu king, Cetewayo, was restored to the throne in 1883 in the ceremony shown in this engraving. King Cetewayo can be distinguished from his subjects by his European-style clothes.

making the Afrikaner consciousness. It was the beginning of a long period during which Anglo-Saxon and Boer struggled to live sometimes apart, sometimes together, but always uncomfortably, their decisions as they did so dragging in their train others about the fate of the black African.

THE EXTENSION OF BRITISH TERRITORY

A Boer republic in Natal was soon made a British colony, in order to protect the Africans from exploitation, and prevent the establishment of a Dutch port which might some day

Paul Kruger, President of the Boer Republic of Transvaal from 1883 to 1900, is portrayed in this 19th-century engraving. Kruger led the Boers into war with Britain (1899–1902).

be used by a hostile power to threaten British communications with the Far East. Another exodus of Boers followed, this time north of the Vaal River. This was the first extension of British territory in South Africa but set a pattern which was to be repeated. Besides humanitarianism, the British government and the British colonists on the spot were stirred by the need to establish good relations with African peoples which would otherwise (as the Zulus had already shown against the Boers) present a continuing security problem (not unlike that posed by Indians in the American colonies in the previous century). By mid-century, there existed two Boer republics in the north (the Orange Free State and the Transvaal), while Cape Colony and Natal were under the British flag, with elected assemblies for which the few black men who met the required economic tests could vote. There were also native states under British protection. In one of these, Basutoland, this actually placed Boers under black jurisdiction, an especially galling subjection for them.

Happy relations were unlikely in these circumstances and, in any case, British governments were often in disagreement with the colonists at the Cape, who, after 1872, had responsible government of their own. New facts arose, too. The discovery of diamonds led to the British annexation of another piece of territory which, since it lay north of the Orange, angered the Boers. British support for the Basutos, whom the Boers had defeated, was a further irritant. Finally, the governor of Cape Colony committed an act of folly by annexing the Transvaal republic. After a successful Boer rising and a nasty defeat of a British force, the British government had the sense not to persist and restored independence to the republic in 1881, but from this moment Boer distrust of British policy in South Africa was probably insurmountable.

THE BOER WAR

Within twenty years of the restoration of independence, tension between the Boers and the British led to war, largely because of two further unanticipated changes. One was a small-scale industrial revolution in the Transvaal republic, where gold was found in 1886. The result was a huge influx of miners and speculators, the involvement of outside financial interests in the affairs of South Africa, and the possibility that the Afrikaner State might have the financial resources to escape from the British suzerainty it unwillingly accepted. The index of what had happened was Johannesburg, which grew in a few years to a city of 100,000 – the only one in Africa south of the Zambezi. The second change was that other parts of Africa were being swallowed in the 1880s and 1890s by other European powers and the British government was reacting by stiffening in its determination that nothing must shake the British presence at the Cape, deemed essential to the control of sea-routes to the East and increasingly dependent on traffic to and from the Transvaal for its revenues. The general effect was to make British governments view with concern any possibility of the Transvaal obtaining independent access to the Indian Ocean. This concern made them vulnerable to the pressure of an oddly assorted crew of idealistic imperialists, Cape politicians, English demagogues and shady financiers who provoked a confrontation with the Boers in 1899 which ended in an ultimatum from the Transvaal's president, Paul Kruger, and the outbreak of the Boer War. Kruger had a deep dislike of the British; as a boy he had gone north on the Great Trek.

This contemporary engraving shows Boer troops attacking a British armour-plated train in 1899.

BRITISH VICTORY AND CONCESSIONS TO THE BOERS

The well-known traditions of the British army of Victorian times were amply sustained in the last war of the reign, both in the level of ineptness and incompetence shown by some higher commanders and administrative services and in the gallantry shown by regimental officers and their men in the face of a brave and well-armed enemy whom their training did not prepare them to defeat. But of the outcome there could be no doubt; as the queen herself remarked, with better strategical judgment than some of her subjects, the possibilities of defeat did not exist. South Africa was a theatre isolated by British sea-power; no other European nation could help the Boers and it was only a matter of time before greatly superior numbers and resources were brought to bear upon them. This cost a great deal – over a quarter of a million soldiers were sent to South Africa –

and aroused much bitterness in British domestic politics; further, it did not present a very favourable picture to the outside world. The Boers were regarded as an oppressed nationality; so they were, but the nineteenth-century liberal obsession with nationality in this case as in others blinded observers to some of the shadows it cast. Fortunately, British statesmanship recovered itself sufficiently to make a generous treaty to end the war in 1902 when the Boers had been beaten in the field. This was the end of the Boer republics. But concession rapidly followed; by 1906 the Transvaal had a responsible government of its own which in spite of the large non-Boer population brought there by mining, the Boers controlled after an electoral victory the following year. Almost at once they began to legislate against Asian immigrants, mainly Indian. (One young Indian lawyer, Mohandas Gandhi, now entered politics as the champion of his community.) When, in 1909, a draft constitution for a

South African Union was agreed, it was on terms of equality for the Dutch and English languages and, all-important, it provided for government by an elected assembly to be formed according to the electoral regulations decided in each province. In the Boer provinces the franchise was confined to white men.

At the time, there was much to be said for the settlement. When people then spoke of a "racial problem" in South Africa they meant the problem of relations between the British and Boers whose conciliation seemed the most urgent need. The defects of the settlement would take some time to appear. When they did it would be not only because the historical sense of the Afrikaner proved to be tougher than people had hoped, but also because the transformation of South African society which had begun by the industrialization of the Rand could not be halted and would give irresistible momentum to the issue of the black Africans.

RESOURCES IN THE BRITISH DOMINIONS

In its economic development, South Africa's future had been just as decisively influenced as had those of all the other British white dominions by being caught up in the trends of the whole world economy. Canada, like the United States, had become with the building of the railroads on her plains one of the great granaries of Europe. Australia and New Zealand first exploited their huge pastures to produce the wool for which European factories were increasingly in the market; then, with the invention of refrigeration, they used them for meat and, in the case of New Zealand, dairy produce. In this way these new nations found staples able to sustain economies much greater than those permitted

by the tobacco and indigo of the seventeenth-century plantations. The case of South Africa was to be different in that she was to reveal herself only gradually (as much later would Australia) as a producer of minerals. The beginning of this was the diamond industry, but the great step forward was the Rand gold discovery of the 1880s. The exploitation of this sucked in capital and expertise to make possible the eventual exploitation of other minerals. The return which South Africa provided was not merely in the profits of European companies and shareholders, but also an augmentation of the world's gold supply which stimulated European commerce much as had done the California discoveries of 1849.

THE TREATMENT OF NATIVE POPULATIONS

THE GROWTH OF HUMANITARIAN and missionary sentiment in England and the well-founded Colonial Office tradition of distrust of settler demands made it harder to forget the native populations of the white dominions than it had been for Americans to

Prospectors are depicted filtering the soil on a river bank in this 19th-century illustration of a diamond field in Britain's South African Cape Colony.

A Maori chief and his wife are portrayed in this engraving dating from the mid-19th century. The Maoris of New Zealand, who were of Polynesian origin, were more adaptable, had more advanced technology and were more warlike than the Australian Aborigines.

into violence by the uncomprehending brutality of the white Australians, and new diseases cut fast into their numbers. The early decades of each Australian colony are stained by the blood of massacred Aborigines; the later years are notorious for the neglect, bullying and exploitation of the survivors. There is perhaps no other population inside former British territory which underwent a fate so like that of the American Indian. In New Zealand, the arrival of the first white men brought guns to the Maori, who employed them first on one another, with disruptive effects upon their societies. Later came the wars with the government, whose essential origin lay in the settlers' displacement of the Maori from their lands. At their conclusion, the government took steps to outlaw the most fraudulent tactics of land acquisition, but the introduction of English notions of individual ownership led to the disintegration of the tribal holdings and the virtual loss of their lands by the end of the century. The Maoris, too, declined in numbers, but not so violently or irreversibly as did the Australian Aborigines. There are now many more Maoris than in 1900 and their numbers grow faster than those of New Zealanders of European stock.

As for South Africa, the story is a mixed one. British protection enabled some of its native peoples to survive into the twentieth century on their ancestral lands living lives which changed only slowly. Others were driven off or exterminated. In all cases, though, the crux of the situation was that in South Africa, as elsewhere, the fate of the native inhabitants was never in their own hands. They depended for their survival upon the local balance of governmental interest and benevolence, settler needs and traditions, economic opportunities and exigencies. Although in the short run they could sometimes present formidable military problems

sweep aside the Plains Indians. Yet in the British colonies, modernity made its impact not upon ancient civilizations but on primitive societies, some of which were at a very low stage of achievement indeed, Neolithic if not Palaeolithic, and correspondingly vulnerable. The Canadian Indians and Eskimos were relatively few and presented no such important obstacle to the exploitation of the west and north-west as had done the Plains Indians' struggle to keep their hunting-grounds. The story in Australia was far bloodier. The hunting and gathering society of the Aborigines was disrupted by settlement, tribes were antagonized and provoked

In this scene from the mid-19th century, Australian Aborigines perform a ceremonial dance. When the British arrived in Australia, it was inhabited by several hundred thousand Aborigines who survived by hunting and gathering. By the beginning of the 20th century the Aborigines' numbers had been reduced to 50,000.

(as did the Zulus of Cetewayo, or the guerrilla warfare of the Maoris) they could not in the end generate from their own resources the means of effective resistance any more than had the Aztecs been able successfully to resist Cortés. For non-European peoples to do that, they would have to Europeanize. The price of establishing the new European nations beyond the seas always turned out to be paid by the native inhabitants, often to the limit of their ability.

EUROPEAN SELF-JUSTIFICATION

The damage done to the aboriginal peoples under their rule by Europeans should not be quite the last word about colonialism. There remains the problem of self-justification: Europeans witnessed the disruption and, often, destruction of native societies and did not stop it. It is too simple to explain this by saying they were all bad, greedy individuals

(and, in any case, the work of the humanitarians among them makes the blackest judgment untenable). The answer must lie somewhere in mentality. Many Europeans who could recognize that the native populations were damaged, even when the white contact with them was benevolent in intention, could not be expected to understand the corrosive effect of this culture on established structures. This requires an anthropological knowledge and insight Europe had still to achieve. It was all the more difficult when, clearly, a lot of native culture was simple savagery and the Europeans' missionary confidence was strong. They *knew* they were on the side of Progress and Improvement, and many still saw themselves as on the side of the Cross, too. This was a confidence which ran through every side of European expansion, the white settler colonies, directly ruled possessions or the arrangements made with dependent societies. The confidence in belonging to a higher civilization was not only a licence for predatory habits as Christianity had earlier been, but the nerve of an attitude akin, in many cases, to that of crusaders. It was their sureness that they brought something better that blinded Europeans all too often to the actual and material results of substituting individual freehold for tribal rights, of turning the hunters and gatherers, whose possessions were what they could carry, into wage-earners.

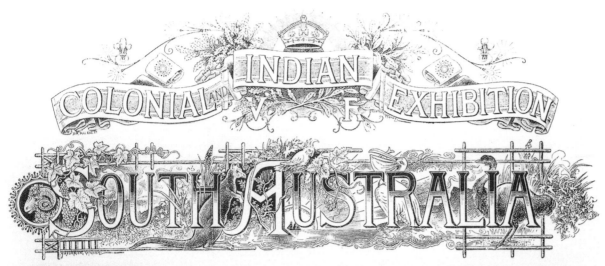

This engraving from the English *Illustrated London News* shows Queen Victoria (1819–1901) visiting the South Australia Exhibit at the Colonial and Indian Exhibition in May 1886.

2 EUROPEAN IMPERIALISM AND IMPERIAL RULE

THE RULING OF ALIEN PEOPLES and other lands by Europeans was the most striking evidence that they ran the world. In spite of enormous argument about what imperialism was and is, it seems helpful to confine the notion of it in the first place to such direct and formal overlordship, blurred though its boundaries with other forms of power over the non-European world may be. This does not raise or answer questions about causes or motives, on which much time, ink and thought have been spent. From the outset different and changing causes were at work, and not all the motives involved were unavowable or self-deceiving. Nor was imperialism the manifestation of only one age, for it has gone on all through history; nor was it peculiar to Europe's relations with non-Europeans overseas, for imperial rule had advanced overland as well as across the seas and some Europeans have ruled others and some non-Europeans Europeans. None the less, in the nineteenth and twentieth centuries the word came to be particularly associated with European expansion and the direct domination of Europeans over the rest of the world had by then become much more obvious than ever before. Although events in the Americas early in the nineteenth century suggested that the European empires built up over the preceding three centuries were in decline, in the next hundred years European imperialism was carried further and became more effective than ever before. This happened in two distinguishable phases, and one running down to about 1870 can conveniently be considered first. Some of the old imperial powers then continued to enlarge their empires impressively; such were Russia, France and Great Britain. Others stood still or found theirs reduced; these were the Dutch, Spanish and Portuguese.

A French expedition crosses the Tonkin mountains, in Indo-China in 1884. The armed escort is made up entirely of natives.

RUSSIAN EXPANSION

The Russian expansion has at first sight something in common both with the American experience of filling up the North American continent and dominating its weaker neighbours, and something with that of the British in India, but was in fact a very special case. To the west Russia faced matured, established European states where there was little hope of successful territorial gain. The same was only slightly less true of expansion into the Turkish territories of the Danubian regions, for here the interests of

Imperialism

Imperialism – the rule, often originating in armed conquest, of one people over others – has existed since the beginning of the first civilizations, in various parts of the world. The term imperialism, however, only came into use in the second half of the 19th century, as a label for the great European colonial expansion that was then taking place.

In the on-going debate about the causes of imperialism, some historians have proposed political explanations, such as the need to divert public attention from domestic problems and gain international prestige. Others favour economic causes – many 19th-century imperialists believed, often erroneously, that empires provided lucrative markets. Some claim that imperialists are motivated by psychological and social issues. Social Darwinism, the once popular theory that Europeans are naturally superior to other races and have a duty to rule over them, was often cited by empire-builders. But many empires have grown from simple international rivalry.

A review of the native cavalry in French Indo-China, in August 1903 is shown. For the most part, order in the colonies was maintained by native troops, organized in European military units and under the command of European officers.

other powers were always likely to come into play against Russia and check her in the end. Her main freedom of action lay southwards and eastwards; in both directions the first three-quarters of the nineteenth century brought great acquisitions. A successful war against Persia (1826–8) led to the establishment of Russian naval power on the Caspian as well as gains of territory in Armenia. In Central Asia an almost continuous advance into Turkestan and towards the central oases of Bokhara and Khiva culminated in the annexation of the whole of Transcaspia in 1881. In Siberia, aggressive expansion was followed by the exaction of the left bank of the Amur down to the sea from China and the founding in 1860 of Vladivostok, the Far Eastern capital. Soon after, Russia liquidated her commitments in America by selling Alaska to the United States; this seemed to show she sought to be an Asian and Pacific, but not an American, power.

THE ERA OF BRITISH NAVAL SUPREMACY

The other two dynamic imperial states of this era besides Russia, France and Great Britain, expanded overseas. Yet many of the Britain gains were made at the expense of France; the Revolutionary and Napoleonic Wars were in this respect the final round of the great colonial Anglo-French contest of the eighteenth century. As in 1714 and 1763, many of Great Britain's acquisitions at a victorious peace in 1815 were intended to reinforce her maritime strength. Malta, St Lucia, the Ionian Islands, the Cape of Good Hope, Mauritius and Trincomalee were all kept for this reason. As steamships took their station in the Royal Navy, the situation of bases had to take coaling into account; this could lead to further acquisitions. In 1839, an internal upheaval in the Ottoman Empire gave the British the opportunity to take Aden, a base of strategic commercial power undertake a policing of the seas from which all could benefit.

Naval supremacy guarded the trade which gave the British colonies participation in the fastest-growing commercial system of the age. Already before the American Revolution British policy had been more encouraging to commercial enterprise than the Spanish or French. Thus the old colonies themselves had grown in wealth and prosperity and the later dominions were to benefit. On the other hand, settlement colonies went out of fashion in London after the American Revolution; they were seen mainly as sources of trouble and expense. Yet Great Britain was the only European country sending out new settlers to existing colonies in the early nineteenth century, and those colonies sometimes drew the mother country into yet further extensions of territorial rule over alien lands.

BRITISH IMPERIAL RULE IN INDIA

IN SOME BRITISH ACQUISITIONS (notably in South Africa) there can be seen at work a new concern about imperial communication with Asia. This is a complicated business. No doubt American independence and the Monroe doctrine diminished the attractiveness of the western hemisphere as a region of imperial expansion, but the origins of a shift of British interest to the East can be seen before 1783, in the opening up of the South Pacific and in a growing Asian trade. War with the Netherlands, when it was a French satellite, subsequently led to new British enterprise in Malaya and Indonesia. Above all, there was the steadily deepening British involvement in India. By 1800 the importance of the Indian trade was already a central axiom of British commercial and colonial thinking. By 1850, it has been urged, much of

Victoria, Queen of England, is depicted with her daughter Princess Beatrice in 1880. The British Empire reached its height during Victoria's long reign (1837–1901). In 1876 she was crowned Empress of India.

importance on the route to India, and others were to follow. No power could successfully challenge such action after Trafalgar. It was not that resources did not exist elsewhere which, had they been assembled, could have wrested naval supremacy form Great Britain. But to do so would have demanded a huge effort. No other nation operated either the number of ships or possessed the bases which could make it worth while to challenge this thalassocracy. There were advantages to other nations in having the world's greatest the rest of the empire had only been acquired because of the strategical needs of India. By then, too, the extension of British control inside the subcontinent itself was virtually complete. It was and remained the centrepiece of British imperialism.

This had hardly been expected or even foreseeable. In 1784 the institution of "Dual Control" had been accompanied by decisions to resist further acquisition of Indian territory; the experience of American rebellion had reinforced the view that new commitments were to be avoided. Yet there was a continuing problem, for through its revenue management the Company's affairs inevitably became entangled in native administration and politics. This made it more important than ever to prevent excesses by its individual officers such as had been tolerable in the early days of private trading; slowly, agreement emerged that the government of India was not only of interest to Parliament because it might be a great source of patronage, but also

because the government in London had a responsibility for the good government of Indians. There began to be articulated a notion of trusteeship. It is perhaps hardly surprising that, during a century in which the idea that government should be for the benefit of the governed was gaining ground in Europe, the same principle should be applied, sooner or later, to rule over colonial peoples. Since the days of Las Casas, exploitation of indigenous peoples had its vociferous critics. In the mid-eighteenth century, a bestselling book by the *abbé* Raynal (it went through thirty editions and many translations in twenty years) had put the criticisms of the churchmen into the secular terms of enlightenment humanitarianism. Against this deep background Edmund Burke in 1783 put it to the House of Commons in a debate on India that "all political power which is set over men … ought to be some way or other exercised ultimately for their benefit".

The influence of British colonization is already evident in this street in Mandalay, Upper Burma, in 1887.

Soldiers from a Bengal infantry regiment are shown taking the town of Minhla in Burma in this engraving, which is dated 1886. In the same year, the British annexed Upper Burma, thus completing their conquest of the country.

Warren Hastings, governor-general of India from 1773 to 1784, was tried by the House of Lords for corruption after his resignation from the post. Corruption was then endemic among British officials in India, although Hastings himself was eventually absolved of the charge.

NEW ATTITUDES TO INDIAN AFFAIRS

The background against which Indian affairs were considered was changing. Across two centuries, the awe and amazement inspired by the Moghul court in the first merchants to reach it had given way rapidly to contempt for what was seen on closer acquaintance as backwardness, superstition and inferiority. But now there were signs of another change. While Clive, the victor of Plassey, never learnt to speak with readiness in any Indian tongue, Warren Hastings, the first governor-general of India, strove to get a chair of Persian set up at Oxford, and encouraged the introduction of the first printing-press to India and the making of the first fount of a vernacular (Bengali) type. There was greater appreciation of the complexity and variety of Indian culture. In 1789 there began to be published in Calcutta the first journal of oriental studies, *Asiatick Researches*. Meanwhile, at the more practical level of government, Company judges were already enjoined to follow Islamic law in family cases involving Muslims, while the revenue authority of Madras both regulated and funded Hindu temples and festivals. From 1806 Indian languages were taught at the Company's college, Haileybury.

The periodic renewals of the Company's charter took place, therefore, in the light of changing influences and assumptions about Anglo-Indian relationships. Meanwhile, government's responsibilities grew. In 1813 renewal strengthened London's control further, and abolished the Company's monopoly of trade with India. By then, the wars with France had already led to the extension of British power over south India through annexation and the negotiation of treaties with native rulers which secured control of their foreign policy. By 1833, when the charter was again renewed, the only important block of territory not ruled directly or indirectly by the Company was in the north-west. The annexation of the Punjab and Sind followed in the 1840s and with their paramountcy established in Kashmir, the British held sway over virtually the whole subcontinent.

THE EAST INDIA COMPANY GOVERNS

The East India Company had ceased to be a commercial organization and had become a government. The 1833 charter took away its trading functions (not only those with India but the monopoly of trade with China); in sympathy with current thinking, Asian trade was henceforth to be conducted on a free trade basis, and the Company confined to an administrative role. The way was open to the consummation of many real and symbolic breaks with India's past and the final incorporation of the subcontinent in a modernizing world. Symbolically, the name of the Moghul emperor was removed from the coinage, but it was more than a symbol that Persian ceased to be the legal language of record and justice. This step not only marked the advance of English as the official language (and therefore of English education), but also disturbed the balance of forces between Indian communities. Anglicized Hindus would prove to do better than less enterprising Muslims. In a subcontinent so divided in so many ways, the adoption of English as the language of administration was complemented by the important decision to provide primary education through instruction given in English.

At the same time an enlightened despotism exercised by successive governors-general began to impose material and institutional improvement. Roads and canals were built and the first railway followed in 1853. Legal codes were introduced. English officials for the Company's service began to be trained specially in the college established for this purpose. The first three universities in India were founded in 1857 and were based on institutions already founded well before this. There were other educational structures, too; as far back as 1791 a Scotchman had founded a Sanskrit college at Benares, the Lourdes of Hinduism. Much of the transformation which India was gradually undergoing arose not from the direct work of government but from the increasing freedom with which these and other agencies were allowed to operate. From 1813 the arrival of missionaries (the Company had hitherto kept them out) gradually built up another constituency at home with a stake in what happened in India – often to the embarrassment of official India. Two philosophies, in effect, were competing to make government act positively. Utilitarianism looked for the promotion of happiness, evangelical Christianity to the salvation of souls. Both

were sure they knew what was best for India and both were equally arrogant in their judgments of it. Both subtly changed British attitudes as time passed.

THE EXPATRIATE COMMUNITY

The coming of the steamship was influential, in that it brought India nearer. More English and Scotch people began to live in India and make their careers there. This gradually transformed the nature of the British presence. The comparatively few officers of the eighteenth-century Company had been content to live the lives of exiles, seeking rewards in their commercial opportunities and relaxation in a social life sometimes closely integrated with that of the Indians. They often lived much in the style of Indian gentlemen, some of them taking to Indian dress and food, some to Indian wives and concubines. Reform-minded officials, intent on the eradication of the backward and barbaric in native practice –

Hider Ali-Khan, Muslim prince of Mysore, is shown receiving the French admiral Pierre de Suffren in 1782. Their collaboration in the struggle against Hastings' British forces failed to save them from defeat.

This 18th-century Indian miniature depicts the maharaja Ranjit Singh (1780–1839), also known as "the Lion of the Punjab", who succeeded his father as a minor Sikh leader in 1792. With the help of an army trained by Western soldiers (the maharaja was a firm ally of the British), Ranjit Singh captured Lahore in 1799 and created a very powerful independent Sikh state in the Punjab region.

English officials and their wives mingle at a tennis party in 19th-century India. Most of the Indians in the picture are servants rather than guests. The English participants' clothes, the furniture and the event itself all signify a determination on the part of the colonialists to cling to the British way of life.

and in such practices as female infanticide and suttee they had good cause for concern – missionaries with a creed to preach which was corrosive of the whole structure of Hindu or Muslim society and, above all, the Englishwomen who arrived to make homes in India for two or three years at a time while their husbands worked there, all changed the temper of the British community. The British in India lived more and more apart from the natives, more and more convinced of their superiority and that it sanctioned the ruling of Indians who were (they felt) culturally and morally inferior. They grew consciously more alien from those they ruled. One of them spoke approvingly of his countrymen as representatives of a "belligerent civilization" and defined their task as "the introduction of the essential parts of European civilization into a country densely peopled, grossly ignorant, steeped in idolatrous superstition, unenergetic, fatalistic, indifferent to most of what we regard as the evils of life and preferring the response of submitting to them to the trouble of encountering and trying to remove them". This robust creed was far from that of the Englishmen of the previous century. They

had innocently sought to do no more in India than make money. Now, while new laws antagonized powerful native interests, those who shared this creed had less and less social contact with Indians; more and more they confined the educated Indian to the lower ranks of the administration and withdrew into an enclosed, but conspicuously privileged, life of their own. Earlier conquerors had been absorbed by Indian society in greater or lesser measure; the Victorian British, thanks to a modern technology which continuously renewed their contacts with the homeland and their confidence in their intellectual and religious superiority, remained immune, increasingly aloof, as no earlier conqueror had been. They could not be untouched by India, as many legacies to the English language and the English breakfast and dinner table still testify, but they created a civilization that was not Indian, even if it was not wholly English; "Anglo-Indian" in the nineteenth century was a word applied not to a person of mixed blood, but to an Englishman who made his career in India, and it indicated a cultural and social distinctiveness.

The mythology of the Mutiny is depicted in this 19th-century engraving of a battle between British and Indian troops.

THE INDIAN MUTINY

THE SEPARATENESS of Anglo-Indian society from India was made virtually absolute by the appalling damage done to British confidence by the rebellions of 1857 called the Indian Mutiny. Essentially, this was a chain reaction of outbreaks, initiated by a mutiny of Hindu soldiers who feared the polluting effect of using a new type of cartridge, greased with animal fat. This detail is significant. Much of the rebellion was the spontaneous and reactionary response of traditional society to innovation and modernization. By way of reinforcement there were the irritations of native rulers, both Muslim and Hindu, who regretted the loss of their privileges and thought that the chance might have come to recover their independence; the British were after all very few. The response of those few was prompt and ruthless. With the help of loyal Indian soldiers the rebellions were crushed, though not before there had been some massacres of British captives and a British force had been under siege at Lucknow, in rebel territory, for some months.

THE MUTINY'S MYTHICAL IMPORTANCE

The Mutiny and its suppression were disasters for British India, though not quite unmitigated. It did not much matter that the Moghul Empire was at last formally brought to an end by the British (the Delhi mutineers had proclaimed the last emperor their leader). Nor was there, as later Indian nationalists were to suggest, a crushing of a national liberation movement whose end was a tragedy for India. Like many episodes important in the making of nations, the Mutiny was to be important as a myth and an inspiration; what it was later believed to have been was more important than what it actually was, a jumble of essentially reactionary protests. Its really disastrous and important effect was the wound it gave to British goodwill and confidence. Whatever the expressed intentions of British policy, the consciousness of the British in India was from this time suffused by the memory that Indians had once proved almost fatally untrustworthy. Among Anglo-Indians as well as Indians the mythical importance of the Mutiny grew with time. The atrocities actually committed were bad enough, but unspeakable ones which had never occurred were also alleged as grounds for a policy of repression and social exclusiveness. Immediately and institutionally, the Mutiny also marked an epoch because it ended the government of the Company. The governor-general now became the queen's viceroy, responsible to a British cabinet minister. This structure provided the framework of the British Raj for the whole of its life.

TRADE

The Mutiny changed Indian history only by thrusting it more firmly in a direction to which it already tended. Another fact which was equally revolutionary for India was much more gradual in its effects. This was the nineteenth-century flowering of the economic connexion with Great Britain. Commerce was the root of the British presence in the subcontinent and it continued to shape its destiny. The first major development came when India became the essential base for the China trade. Its greatest expansion came in the 1830s and 1840s when, for a number of reasons, access to China became much easier. It was at about the same time that there took place the first rapid rise in British exports to India, notably of textiles, so that, by the time of the Mutiny, a big Indian commercial interest existed which involved many more Englishmen and

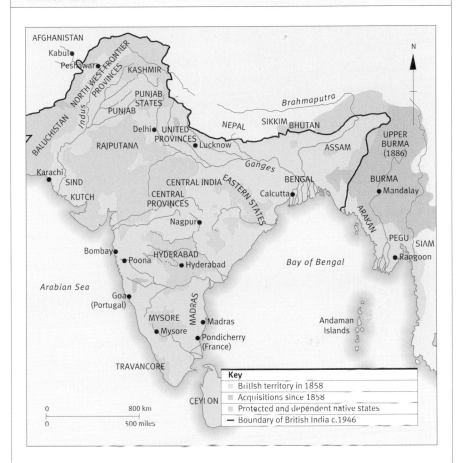

British India

Once the rebellions of the Indian Mutiny had been quashed in 1858, the old British East India Company was dissolved and India became a direct dominion of the British Crown.

However, the Indian principalities, ruled independently by their princes, survived until the end of the colonial period, although they were subject to British protectorate.

English commercial houses than the old Company had ever done.

The story of Anglo-Indian trade was now locked into that of the general expansion of British manufacturing supremacy and world commerce. The Suez Canal brought down the costs of shipping goods to Asia by a huge factor. By the end of the century the volume of British trade with India had more than quadrupled. The effects were felt in both countries, but were decisive in India, where a check was imposed on an industrialization which might have gone ahead more rapidly without British competition. Paradoxically, the growth of trade thus delayed India's modernization and alienation from its own past. But there were other forces at work, too. By the end of the century the framework provided by the Raj and the stimulus of the cultural influences it permitted had already made impossible the survival of wholly unmodernized India.

FRENCH IMPERIALISM

No OTHER NATION in the early nineteenth century so extended its imperial possessions as Great Britain, but the French, too, had made substantial additions to the empire with which they had been left in 1815. In the next half-century France's interests elsewhere (in West Africa and the South Pacific, for example) were not lost to sight but the first clear sign of a reviving French imperialism came in Algeria. The whole of North Africa was open to imperial expansion by European predators because of the decay of the formal overlordship of the Ottoman sultan. Right round the southern and eastern Mediterranean coasts the issue was posed of a possible Turkish partition. French interest in the area was natural; it went back to a great extension of the country's Levant trade in the eighteenth century and an expedition to Egypt under Bonaparte in 1798.

Algeria's conquest began uncertainly in 1830. A series of wars not only with its native inhabitants but with the sultan of Morocco followed until, by 1870, most of the country had been subdued. This was, in fact, to open a new phase of expansion, for the French then turned their attention to Tunis, which accepted a French protectorate in 1881. To both these sometime Ottoman dependencies there now began a steady flow of European

This picture was painted in 1834 by the French artist Emile Vernet. Entitled *Arab Chiefs Meeting in Council*, it shows a scene from the French conquest of Algeria.

immigrants, not only from France, but from Italy and, later, Spain. This built up substantial settler populations in a few cities which were to complicate the story of French rule. The day was past when the African Algerians might have been exterminated or all but exterminated, like the Aztecs, American Indians or Australian Aborigines. Their society, in any case, was more resistant, formed in the crucible of an Islamic civilization which had once contested Europe so successfully. None the less, they suffered, notably from the introduction of land law which broke up their traditional usages and impoverished the peasants by exposing them to the full blast of market economics.

EGYPT

At the eastern end of the African littoral a national awakening in Egypt led to the emergence there of the first great modernizing nationalist leader outside the European world, Mehemet Ali, pasha of Egypt. Admiring Europe, he sought to borrow its ideas and techniques while asserting his independence of the sultan. When he was later called upon for help by the sultan against the Greek revolution, Mehemet Ali went on to attempt to seize Syria as his reward. This threat to the Ottoman Empire provoked an international crisis in the 1830s in which the French took his side. They were not successful, but thereafter French policy continued to interest itself in the Levant and Syria, too, an interest which was eventually to bear fruit in the brief establishment in the twentieth century of a French presence in the area.

THE LAST IMPERIAL WAVE

The feeling that Great Britain and France had made good use of their opportunities in the

early part of the nineteenth century was no doubt one reason why other powers tried to follow them from 1870 onwards. But envious emulation does not go far as an explanation of the extraordinary suddenness and vigour of what has sometimes been called the "imperialist wave" of the late nineteenth century. Outside Antarctica and the Arctic less than a fifth of the world's land surface was not under a European flag or that of a country of European settlement by 1914; and of this small fraction only Japan, Ethiopia and Siam enjoyed real autonomy.

Why this happened has been much debated. Clearly one part of the story is that of the sheer momentum of accumulated forces. The European hegemony became more and more irresistible as it built upon its own strength. The theory and ideology of imperialism were up to a point mere rationalizations of the huge power the European world suddenly found itself to possess. Practically, for example, as medicine began to master tropical infection and steam provided quicker transport, it became easier to establish permanent bases in Africa and to penetrate its interior; the Dark Continent had long been of interest but its exploitation

The French infantry shoot at a band of retreating Algerian horsemen in November 1836. In spite of their apparent military superiority, however, the 1836 campaign was a disaster for the French.

began to be feasible for the first time in the 1870s. Such technical developments made possible and attractive a spreading of European rule which could promote and protect trade and investment. The hopes such possibilities aroused were often ill-founded and usually disappointed. Whatever the appeal of "undeveloped estates" in Africa (as one British statesman liked to put it), or the supposedly vast market for consumer goods constituted by the penniless millions of China, industrial countries still found other industrial countries their best customers and trading partners and it was former or existing colonies rather than new ones which attracted most overseas capital investment. By far the greatest part of British money invested abroad went to the United States and South America; French investors preferred Russia to Africa, and German money went to Turkey.

IMPERIAL RIVALRY

Economic expectation excited many individuals. Because of them, imperial expansion always had a random factor in it which makes it hard to generalize about. Explorers, traders and adventurers on many occasions took steps which led governments, willingly or not, to seize more territory. They were often popular heroes, for this most active phase of European imperialism coincided with a great growth of popular participation in public affairs. By buying newspapers, voting, or cheering in the streets, the masses were more and more involved in politics which (among other things) emphasized imperial competition as a form of national rivalry. The new cheap press often pandered to this by dramatising exploration and colonial warfare. Some thought, too, that social dissatisfactions might be soothed by the contemplation of the extension of the rule of the

The "burden" of colonialism

The English author Rudyard Kipling (1865–1936) wrote a well-known exaltation of colonialism, which he portrayed as a burden taken on by the colonizers for the benefit of the colonized, in a poem in which he exhorted the United States to take on this role in the Philippines. It begins:

"Take up the White Man's Burden–
Send forth the best ye breed–
Go bind your sons to exile
To serve your captives' need;
To wait in heavy harness
On fluttered folk and wild–
Your new-caught, sullen peoples,
Half devil and half child.

"Take up the White Man's Burden–
In patience to abide,
To veil the threat of terror
And check the show of pride;
By open speech and simple,
A hundred times made plain,
To seek another's profit,
And work another's gain.

"Take up the White Man's Burden–
The savage wars of peace–
Fill full the mouth of Famine
And bid the sickness cease;
And when your goal is nearest
The end for others sought,
Watch Sloth and heathen Folly
Bring all your hope to nought."

The first three verses of "The White Man's Burden" by Rudyard Kipling, 1899.

national flag over new areas even when the experts knew that nothing was likely to be forthcoming except expense.

But cynicism is no more the whole story than is the profit motive. The idealism which inspired some imperialists certainly salved the conscience of many more. Those who believed that they possessed true civilization were bound to see the ruling of others for their good as a duty. Kipling's famous poem did not urge Americans to take up the White Man's Booty, but his Burden.

All these elements were tangled together more than ever after 1870. They all had to find a place in a context of changing international relationships which imposed its own logic on colonial affairs. The story need not be explained in detail, but two continuing themes stand out in it. One is that, because she was the only truly worldwide imperial power, Great Britain quarrelled with other states over colonies more than anyone else. She had possessions everywhere. The centre of her concerns was more than ever India; the acquisition of African territory to safeguard the Cape route and the new one via Suez, and frequent alarms over dangers to the lands which were India's glacis both showed this. Between 1870 and 1914 the only crises over non-European issues which made war between Great Britain and another great power seem possible arose over Russian dabblings in Afghanistan and a French attempt to establish themselves on the Upper Nile. British officials were also much concerned about French penetration of West Africa and Indo-China, and Russian influence in Persia.

IMPERIALISM AND EUROPEAN RELATIONS

International disagreements about colonial issues indicate the second continuing theme. Though European nations quarrelled about what happened overseas for forty years or so, and though the United States went to war with one of them (Spain), the partition of the non-European world was amazingly peaceful. When a Great War at last broke out in 1914, Great Britain, Russia and France, the three nations which had quarrelled with one another most over imperial difficulties, would be on the same side; it was not overseas colonial rivalry which caused the conflict. Only once after 1900, in Morocco, did a real danger of war occasioned by a quarrel over non-European lands arise between two European great powers and here the issue was not really one of colonial rivalry, but of whether Germany could bully France without fear of her being supported by others. Quarrels over non-European affairs before 1914 seem in fact to have been a positive distraction from the more dangerous rivalries of Europe itself; they may even have helped to preserve European peace.

Africa in 1880

Key
- British possessions
- French possessions
- Portuguese possessions
- Spanish possessions
- Turkish possessions

In 1880, European presence was limited to narrow coastal strips, with the exception of Algeria and Senegal and the British and the Boers in South Africa. The Turkish dominion over many areas was more theoretical than real. In little more than a decade, the panorama would change drastically, with most of the continent coming under European rule.

Africa in 1914

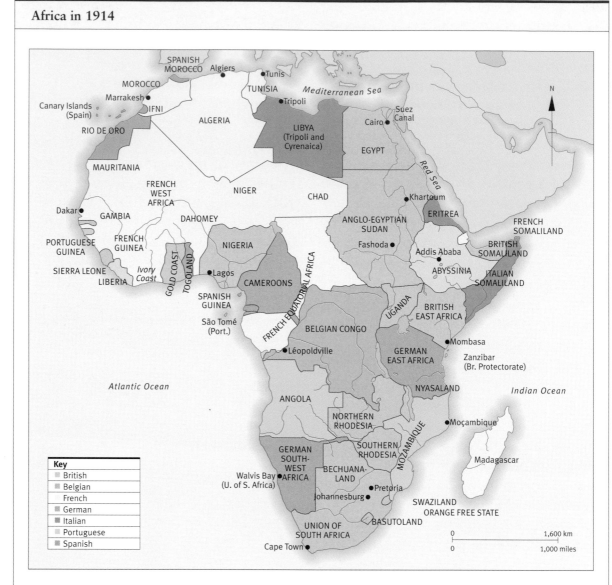

By 1914 all of Africa was under European domination, except for Liberia, which an American society had founded in 1816 as a state in which emancipated slaves could settle, and Abyssinia (Ethiopia), a Christian kingdom which defeated one Italian invasion attempt in 1896, only to succumb to a second in 1936.

THE SCRAMBLE FOR AFRICA

IMPERIAL RIVALRY had its own momentum. When a power got a new concession or a colony, it almost always spurred on others to go one better. The imperialist wave was in this way self-feeding. By 1914 the most striking results were to be seen in Africa. The activities of explorers, missionaries, and the campaigners against slavery early in the nineteenth century had encouraged the belief that extension of European rule in the "Dark Continent" was a matter of spreading enlightenment and humanitarianism – the blessings of civilization, in fact. On the African coasts, centuries of trade had shown that desirable products were available in the interior. The whites at the Cape were already pushing further inland (often because of Boer resentment of British rule). Such facts made up an explosive mixture, which was set off in 1881 when a British force was sent to Egypt to secure that country's government against a nationalist revolution whose success (it was feared) might threaten the safety of the Suez Canal. The corrosive power of European culture – for this was the source of the ideas of the Egyptian nationalists – thus both touched off another stage in the decline of the Ottoman Empire of which Egypt was still formally a part and launched what was called the "Scramble for Africa".

THE PARTITION OF AFRICA

The British had hoped to withdraw their soldiers from Egypt quickly; in 1914 they were still there. British officials were by then virtually running the administration of the country while, to the south, Anglo-Egyptian rule had been pushed deep into the Sudan. Meanwhile, Turkey's western provinces in Libya and Tripolitania had been taken by the Italians (who felt unjustly kept out of Tunisia by the French protectorate there), Algeria was French, and the French enjoyed a fairly free hand in Morocco, except where the Spanish were installed. Southwards from Morocco to the Cape of Good Hope, the coastline was entirely divided between the British, French, Germans, Spanish, Portuguese and Belgians, with the exception of the isolated black republic of Liberia. The empty wastes of the Sahara were French; so was the basin of the Senegal and much of the northern side of that of the Congo. The Belgians were installed in the rest of it on what was soon to prove some of the richest mineral-bearing land in Africa. Further east, British territories ran from the Cape up to Rhodesia and the Congo border. On the east coast they were cut off from the sea by Tanganyika (which was German) and Portuguese East Africa. From Mombasa,

Kenya's port, a belt of British territory stretched through Uganda to the borders of the Sudan and the headwaters of the Nile. Somalia and Eritrea (in British, Italian and French hands) isolated Ethiopia, the only African country other than Liberia still independent of European rule. The ruler of this ancient but Christian polity was the only non-European ruler of the nineteenth century to avert the threat of colonization by a military success, the annihilation of an Italian army at Adowa in 1896. Other Africans did not have the power to resist successfully, as the French suppression of Algerian revolt in 1871, the Portuguese mastery (with some difficulty) of insurrection in Angola in 1902 and again in 1907, the British destruction of the Zulu and Matabele, and, worst of all, the German massacre of the Herrero of South West Africa in 1907, all showed.

THE EFFECTS OF COLONIALISM

The colossal extension of European power, for the most part achieved after 1881,

An Egyptian garrison prepares to defend a fortress in Sudan from the approach of Mahdist troops in an engraving dated 1884. Two years earlier, Egypt had become a British protectorate. At that time, Egyptian rule of Sudan, an inheritance from the Ottoman era, was threatened by an uprising led by a religious leader, the Mahdi. He died in 1885 and in 1898, his successor, the Khalifa, was defeated by the British.

This photograph of Adjiki-Toffia, King of Dahomey, was taken in 1908. The king, with his subjects prostrated before him, is wearing a European uniform – his kingdom had been conquered by the French in 1892.

transformed African history. The bargains of European negotiators, the accidents of discovery and the convenience of colonial administrations in the end settled the ways in which modernization came to Africa. The suppression of intertribal warfare and the introduction of even elementary medical services released population growth in some areas. As in America centuries earlier, the introduction of new crops made it possible to feed more people. Different colonial régimes had different cultural and economic impact, however. Long after the colonialists had gone, there would be big distinctions between countries where, say, French administration or British judicial practice had taken root. All over the continent Africans found new patterns of employment, learnt something of European ways through European schools or service in colonial regiments, saw different things to admire or hate in the white man's ways which now came to regulate their lives. Even when, as in some British possessions, great emphasis was placed on rule through traditional native institutions, they had henceforth to work in a new context. Tribal and local unities would go on asserting themselves but more and more did so against the grain of new structures created by colonialism and left as a legacy of independent Africa. Languages, Christian monogamy, entrepreneurial attitudes, new knowledge, all contributed finally to a new self-consciousness and greater individualism. From such influences would emerge the new Africans of the twentieth century. Without imperialism, for good or ill, those influences could never have been so effective so fast.

AFRICA'S IMPACT ON EUROPE

Europe, by contrast, was hardly changed by the African adventure, and it is easy to overestimate its brief effect there. Clearly, it was important that Europeans could lay their hands on yet more easily exploitable wealth, yet probably only Belgium drew from Africa resources making a real difference to its national future. Sometimes, too, the exploiting of Africa aroused political opposition in European countries; there was more than a touch of the conquistadores about some of the late nineteenth-century adventurers. The administration of the Congo by the Belgian king Leopold and forced labour in Portuguese Africa were notorious examples, but there were other places where Africa's natural resources – human and material – were ruthlessly exploited or despoiled in the interests of profit by Europeans with the connivance of imperial authorities, and this soon created an anti-colonial movement. Some nations recruited African soldiers, though not for service in Europe, where only the French hoped to employ them to offset the weight of German numbers. Some countries hoped for outlets for emigration which would ease social problems, but the opportunities presented by Africa for European residence were very mixed. The two large blocks of settlement were in the south, and the British would later open up Kenya and Rhodesia where there were lands suitable for white farmers. Apart from this, there were the cities of French North Africa, and also a growing community of Portuguese in Angola. The hopes entertained of Africa as an outlet for Italians, on the other hand, were disappointed, and German emigration was tiny and almost entirely temporary. Some European countries – Russia, Austria, Hungary and the Scandinavian nations – sent virtually no settlers to Africa at all.

IMPERIALISM IN ASIA AND THE PACIFIC

Of course, there was much more than Africa to the story of nineteenth century imperialism. The Pacific was partitioned less dramatically but in the end no independent political unit survived among its island peoples. There was also a big expansion of British, French and Russian territory in Asia. The French established themselves in Indo-China, the British in Malaya and Burma, which they took to safeguard the approaches to India. Siam retained her independence

Under colonial rule, some aspects of the traditional African way of life remained practically unchanged. These Nubian children, depicted protecting their crops from birds, were painted by the French artist Maurice Berchère.

because it suited both powers to have a buffer between them. The British also asserted their superiority by an expedition to Tibet, with the same considerations of Indian security in mind. Most of these areas, like much of the zone of Russian overland expansion, were formally under Chinese suzerainty. Their story is part of that of the crumbling Chinese Empire, a story which paralleled the corrosion of other empires, such as the Ottoman, Moroccan and Persian, by European influence, though it has even greater importance for world history. At one moment it looked as if a Scramble for China might follow the partition of Africa. That story is better considered elsewhere. Here it is convenient to notice that the imperialist wave in the Chinese sphere as in the Pacific was importantly different from that in Africa because the United States of America took part.

AMERICAN IMPERIALISM

AMERICANS HAD ALWAYS been uneasy and distrustful over imperial ventures outside the continent they long regarded as God-given to them. Even at its most arrogant, imperialism had to be masked, muffled and muted in the republic in a way unnecessary in Europe. The very creation of the United States had been by successful rebellion against an imperialist power. The constitution contained no provision for the ruling of colonial possessions and it was always very difficult to see what could be the position under it of territories which could not be envisaged as eventually moving towards full statehood, let alone that of non-Americans who stayed under American rule. On the other hand, there was much that was barely distinguishable from imperialism in the

In the 19th century, the Pacific islands became a refuge for many Europeans in search of a new life far away from "civilization". The French post-Impressionist painter Paul Gauguin (1848–1903), whose *Tahitian Women at the Beach* is shown here, settled in Tahiti in 1891 and remained there for most of the rest of his life.

The port of Pago Pago, the capital of American Samoa, is depicted in 1886.

nincteenth-century territorial expansion of the United States, though Americans might not recognize it when it was packaged as a "Manifest Destiny". The most blatant examples were the war of 1812 against the British and the treatment of Mexico in the middle of the century. But there was also the dispossession of the Indians to consider and the dominating implications of the Monroe doctrine.

In the 1890s the overland expansion of the United States was complete. It was announced that the continuous frontier of domestic settlement no longer existed. At this moment, economic growth had given great importance to the influence of business interests in American government, sometimes expressed in terms of economic nationalism and high tariff protection. Some of these interests directed the attention of American public opinion abroad, notably to Asia. The United States was thought by some to be in danger of exclusion from trade there by the European powers. There was an old connexion at stake (the first American Far Eastern squadron had been sent out in the 1820s) as a new era of Pacific awareness dawned with California's rapid growth in population. A half-century's talk of a canal across Central America also came to a head at the end of the century; it stimulated interest in the doctrines of strategists who suggested that the United States might need an oceanic glacis in the Pacific to maintain the Monroe doctrine.

RAPID EXPANSION

All these currents flowed into a burst of expansion which has remained to this day a unique example of American overseas imperialism because, for a time, it set aside traditional restraint on the acquisition of new territory overseas. The beginnings must be traced back to the increased opening of China and Japan to American commerce in the 1850s and 1860s and to participation with the British and the Germans in the administration of Samoa (where a naval base obtained in 1878 has remained a United States possession). This was followed by two decades of growing intervention in the affairs of the kingdom of Hawaii, to which the protection of the United States had been extended since the 1840s. American traders and missionaries had established themselves there in large numbers. Benevolent patronage of the Hawaiians gave way to attempts to achieve annexation to the United States in the 1890s. Washington already had the use of

Pearl Harbor as a naval base but was led to land marines in Hawaii when a revolution occurred there. In the end, the government had to give way to the forces set in motion by the settlers and a short-lived Hawaiian Republic was annexed as a United States Territory in 1898.

SPANISH COLONIES FALL TO AMERICA

In 1898, a mysterious explosion destroyed an American cruiser, the USS *Maine*, in Havana harbour. This led to a war with Spain. In the background was both the long Spanish failure to master revolt in Cuba, where American business interests were prominent and American sentiment was aroused, and the growing awareness of the importance of the Caribbean approaches to a future canal across the isthmus. In Asia, American help was given to another rebel movement against the Spaniards in the Philippines. When American rule replaced Spanish in Manila, the rebels turned against their former allies and a guerrilla war began. This was the first phase of a long and difficult process of disentangling the United States from her first Asian colony. At that moment, given the likelihood of the collapse of the Chinese Empire, it seemed best in Washington not to withdraw. In the Caribbean, the long history of Spanish empire in the Americas at last came to an end. Puerto Rico passed to the United States and Cuba obtained its independence on terms which guaranteed its domination by the United States. American forces went back to occupy the island under these terms from 1906 to 1909, and again in 1917.

THE PANAMA CANAL

The end of Spanish rule in the Caribbean was the prelude to the last major development in

American soldiers and native Muslims on the Philippine island of Mindanao are seen in a photograph dating from 1900. Having usurped Spain as the ruling colonial power, the Americans had to face the same guerrillas who had fought against Spain.

this wave of American imperialism. The building of an isthmian canal had been canvassed since the middle of the nineteenth century and the completion of Suez gave it new plausibility. American diplomacy negotiated a way round the obstacle of possible British participation; all seemed plain sailing but a snag arose in 1903 when a treaty providing for the acquisition of a canal zone from Colombia was rejected by the Colombians. A revolution was engineered in Panama, where the canal was to run. The United States prevented its suppression by the Colombian government and a new Panamanian republic emerged which gratefully bestowed upon the United States the necessary territory together with the right to intervene in its affairs to maintain order. The work could now begin and the canal was opened in 1914. The possibility of transferring ships rapidly from one ocean to another made a great difference to American naval strategy. It was also the background to the "corollary" to the Monroe doctrine proposed by President Theodore Roosevelt; when the Canal Zone became the key to the naval defence of the hemisphere, it was more important than ever to assure its protection by stable government and United

The Panama Canal

The Portuguese seafarer Antonio Galvao was the first person to suggest the idea of opening a canal in the Isthmus of Darién in Panama, in a book he wrote in 1550. As for the Suez Canal, it was a group of French financiers who obtained the concession to build a canal which would join Colón on the Atlantic coast to Panama on the Pacific. Ferdinand de Lesseps, the French diplomat who had spearheaded the Suez project, formed the Compagnie Universelle du Canal Interocéanique in 1879. Work began the following year on the canal, but the enterprise, having cost 287 million dollars and more than 20,000 lives, had to be abandoned in 1889 when the company went bankrupt.

In 1903, the United States government supported Panama's independence and obtained in exchange permission to open up the canal. The chief engineer of the US Isthmian Canal Commission, John F. Stevens, drew up the final plans in 1906. He favoured a high-level rather than a sea-level canal – a system of interconnecting lakes and six pairs of enormous locks were built to enable vessels to navigate the 85 ft (26 m) difference between sea level and the level of the highest lake, Lake Gatún.

Although the workers were mainly spared the bouts of malaria and yellow fever that had cursed the French project, technical problems dogged the construction process. The worst of these occurred at the Gaillard Cut, where an 8 mile (12 km) artificial canyon had to be dug through the mountain. Internal

pressure forced the excavated earth upwards and caused landslides in the canyon walls. What was initially planned as a narrow gorge became a huge valley with gently sloping sides.

Since the canal's official opening in 1914, it has been controlled by the United States. Under the terms of the 1977 Treaty of Panama, sovereignty of the canal will pass to the Republic of Panama in the year 2000. It is feared, however, that a recent fall in the volume of water in its tributaries may endanger the canal's system in the coming years.

The SS Ancon *approaches the Cucaracha Slide on 15 August, 1914. The* Ancon *was the first ship to pass through the Panama Canal.*

States predominance in the Caribbean states. A new vigour in American intervention in them was soon evident.

THE COLONIAL WORLD

Though its motives and techniques were different – for one thing, there was virtually no permanent American settlement in the new possessions – the actions of the United States were part of the last great seizure of territories carried out by the European peoples. Almost all of them had taken part except the South Americans; even the Queenslanders had tried to annexe New Guinea. By 1914 a third of the world's surface was under two flags, those of the United Kingdom and Russia (though how much Russian territory should be regarded as colonial is, of course, debatable). To take a measure which excludes Russia, in 1914 the United Kingdom ruled four hundred million subjects outside its own borders, France over fifty million and Germany and Italy about fourteen million each; this was an unprecedented aggregation of formal authority.

At that date, though, there were already signs that imperialism overseas had run out of steam. China had proved a disappointment and there was little left to divide, though Germany and Great Britain discussed the possibility of partitioning the Portuguese Empire, which seemed to be about to follow the Spanish. The most likely area left for further European imperialism was the decaying Ottoman Empire, whose dissolution seemed at last to be imminent when the Italians seized Tripoli in 1912 and a Balkan coalition formed against Turkey took away almost all that was left of her European territories in the following year. Such a prospect did not seem likely to be so free from conflict between great powers as had been the partition of Africa; much more crucial issues would be at stake in it for them.

King George V and Queen Mary of Britain appear on the wall of the Red Fort in Delhi in 1911 during the Coronation Durbar. This was the first visit to India by a reigning British monarch and it was hoped that the dazzling spectacle would revive Indian subjects' loyalty to the Crown. The event failed, however, to curtail the Indian independence movement, which was already well under way.

3 ASIA'S RESPONSE TO A EUROPEANIZING WORLD

A PERCEPTIVE CHINESE OBSERVER might have found something revealing in the disgrace which in the end overtook the Jesuits at K'ang-hsi's court. For more than a century these able men had judiciously and discreetly sought to ingratiate themselves with their hosts. To begin with they had not even spoken of religion, but had contented themselves with studying the language of China. They had even worn Chinese dress, which, we are told, created a very good impression. Great successes had followed. Yet

the effectiveness of their mission was suddenly paralysed; their acceptance of Chinese rites and beliefs and their sinicizing of Christian teaching led to the sending of two papal emissaries to China to check such improper flexibility. This was striking: evidently Europeans, unlike all other conquerors of China, would not easily succumb to its cultural pull. There was a message for all Asia in this revelation of the intransigence of European culture. It was more important to what was going to happen in Asia – and was already under way there – than even the technology of the newcomers. It was certainly more decisive than any temporary or special weaknesses of the Eastern empires, as China's own history was to show. Under the immediate successors of K'ang-hsi, the Manchu Empire was already past its peak; its slow and eventually fatal decline would not have in itself been surprising given the cyclical pattern of dynastic rise and fall in the past. What made the fate of the Ch'ing Dynasty different from that of its predecessors was that it survived long enough to preside over the country while it faced a quite new threat, one from a culture stronger than that of traditional China. For the first time in nearly two thousand years, Chinese society would have to change, not the imported culture of a new wave of barbarian conquerors. The Chinese Revolution was about to begin.

A Ch'ing emperor is depicted in the gardens of his harem. The Ch'ing Dynasty, of Manchu origins, ruled China from 1644 to 1912.

CHINESE CONFIDENCE

In the eighteenth century, no Chinese official could have been expected to predict the eventual decline of the Manchu Empire. When

Lord Macartney arrived in 1793 to ask for equality of diplomatic representation and free trade the confidence of centuries was intact. The first Western advances and encroachments had been successfully rebuffed or contained. The representative of George III could only take back polite but unyielding messages of refusal to what the Chinese emperor was pleased to call "the lonely remoteness of your island, cut off from the world by intervening wastes of sea". It can hardly have improved matters that George was also patted on the back for his "submissive loyalty in sending this tribute mission" and encouraged to "show even greater devotion and loyalty in future".

The assumption of their own cultural and moral superiority was then as unquestioned a part of the mental world of the educated Chinese as it was of that of the European and American missionaries and philanthropists of the next century who unconsciously patronized the people they came to serve. Such language embodied the Chinese world view, in which all nations paid tribute to the emperor, possessed of the Mandate of Heaven, and in which China already had all the materials and skills for the highest civilization and would only waste her time and energy in indulging relations with Europe going beyond the limited trade tolerated at Canton (where by 1800 there were perhaps a thousand Europeans). Nor was this nonsense. Nearly three centuries of trade with China had failed to reveal any manufactured goods from Europe which the Chinese wanted

except the mechanical toys and clocks which they found amusing. European trade with China rested on the export to her of silver or other Asian products. As a British merchant concisely put it in the middle of the eighteenth century, the "East India trade ... exports our bullion, spends little of our product or manufactures and brings in commodities perfectly manufactured which hinder the consumption of our own".

POPULATION PRESSURE AND INFLATION

In the mid-eighteenth century, official China still felt confident about her internal régime

This 19th-century engraving depicts the preparations for a wedding in a luxurious Chinese mansion. Although Western influences were present in many parts of China at the time, they had hardly touched the traditional Chinese way of life.

Time chart (1839–1912)					
		1850–1864 The Taiping Insurrection in China	1885 The Indian National Congress is founded	1899–1900 Boxer Rebellion in China	1911–1912 Chinese Republican revolution
1800			1850		1900
	1839–1842 The first Opium War		1868 "Meiji Restoration" in Japan	1894–1895 Sino-Japanese War	1904–1905 War between Russia and Japan

and cultural superiority, but in retrospect signs of future difficulties can be discerned. The secret societies and cults which kept alive a smouldering national resentment against a foreign dynasty and the central power, still survived and even prospered. They found fresh support as the surge of population became uncontainable; in the century before 1850 numbers seem to have more than doubled to reach about four hundred and thirty million by 1850. Pressure on cultivated land became much more acute because the area worked could be increased only by a tiny margin; times grew steadily harder and the lot of the peasantry more and more miserable. There had been warning signs in the 1770s and 1780s when a century's internal peace was broken by great revolts such as those which had so often in the past been the sign of dynastic decline. Early in the next century they became more frequent and destructive. To make matters worse, they were accompanied by another economic deterioration, inflation in the price of the silver in which taxes had to be paid. Most daily transactions (including the payment of wages) were carried out in copper, so this added to the crushing burdens already suffered by the poor. Yet none of this seemed likely to be

A British ship, the HMS *Leopard*, is pictured in dock at Shanghai in the mid-19th century. The whole Yangtze valley area came under British influence when China was forced to open up to international trade.

fatal, except, possibly, to the dynasty. It could all be fitted into the traditional pattern of the historic cycle. All that was required was that the service gentry should remain loyal, and even if they did not, then, though a collapse of government might follow, there was no reason to believe that in due course another dynasty would not emerge to preserve the imperial framework of an unchanging China.

THE OPIUM WAR

China's historic dynastic cycle, in the end, was broken by the drive and power of the nineteenth-century barbarian challenge. The inflation itself was a result of a change of China's relations with the outside world which within a few decades made nonsense of the reception given to Macartney. Before 1800 the West could offer China little that she wanted except silver, but within the next three decades of the nineteenth century this ceased to be so, largely because British traders at last found a commodity the Chinese wanted and India could supply: opium. Naval expeditions forced the Chinese to open their country to sale (albeit at first under certain restrictions) of this drug, but the "Opium War" which began in 1839 ended in 1842 with a treaty which registered a fundamental change in China's relations with the West. The Canton monopoly and the tributary status of the foreigner came to an end together. Once the British had kicked ajar the door to Western trade, others were to follow them through it.

GROWING SUBVERSION

Unwittingly, the government of Queen Victoria launched the Chinese Revolution. The 1840s were the beginning of a period of

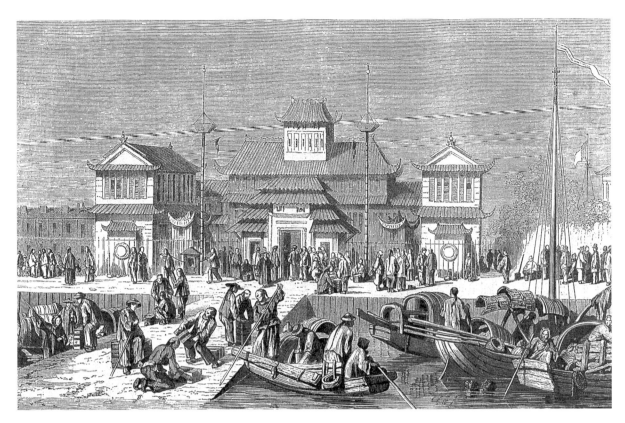

upheaval which took over a century to come to completion. The revolution would slowly reveal itself as a double repudiation, both of the foreigner and of much of the Chinese past. The first would increasingly express itself in the nationalist modes and idioms of the progressive European world. Because such ideological forces could not be contained within the traditional framework, they would in the end prove fatal to it, when the Chinese sought to remove the obstacles to modernization and national power. More than a century after the Opium War the Chinese Revolution at last finally shattered for good a social system which had been the foundation of Chinese life for thousands of years. By that time, though, much of old China would already have vanished. By that time, too, it would appear that China's troubles had also been a part of a much wider upheaval, a Hundred Years' War of Asia and the West whose turning-point came in the early twentieth century.

HOSTILITY TO WESTERNERS

The implications of the growing European influence in China matured only slowly. In the beginning, Western encroachments in China usually produced only a simple, xenophobic hostility and even this was not universal. After all, for a long time very few Chinese were directly or obviously much concerned with the coming of the foreigners. A few (notably Canton merchants involved in the foreign trade) even sought accommodation with them. Hostility was a matter of anti-British mobs in the towns and of the rural gentry. At first many officials saw the problem as a limited one: that of the addiction of the subjects of the empire to a dangerous drug. They were humiliated, in particular, by the weaknesses which this revealed in their own people and administration; there was much connivance and corruption involved in the opium trade. They do not at first seem to have seen the deeper

Manchu China 1644–1912

In 1644, the invasion of China by the Manchus put an end to the Ming Dynasty. The invaders founded the new Ch'ing Dynasty, which was to rule over this vast country for two and a half centuries. It was not long before the Ch'ing emperors were facing Russian pressure on China's northern frontiers. However, the pressure exerted by the rest of the Western world, which increased significantly by the mid-19th century, represented a much greater threat to political stability in Manchu China.

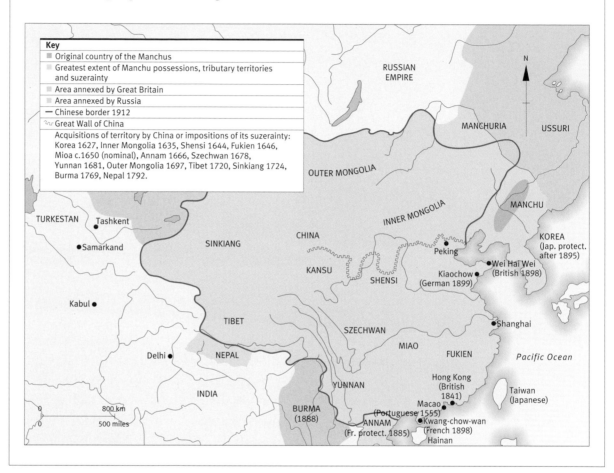

Key
- Original country of the Manchus
- Greatest extent of Manchu possessions, tributary territories and suzerainty
- Area annexed by Great Britain
- Area annexed by Russia
- Chinese border 1912
- Great Wall of China

Acquisitions of territory by China or impositions of its suzerainty: Korea 1627, Inner Mongolia 1635, Shensi 1644, Fukien 1646, Mioa c.1650 (nominal), Annam 1666, Szechwan 1678, Yunnan 1681, Outer Mongolia 1697, Tibet 1720, Sinkiang 1724, Burma 1769, Nepal 1792.

issue of the future, that of the questioning of an entire order, or sense a cultural threat; China had suffered defeats in the past and its culture had survived unscathed.

The first portent of a deeper danger came when, in the 1840s, the imperial government had to concede that missionary activity was legal. Though still limited, this was obviously corrosive of tradition. Officials in the Confucian mould who felt its danger stirred up popular feeling against missionaries – whose efforts made them easy targets – and there were scores of riots in the 1850s and 1860s. Such demonstrations often made things worse. Sometimes foreign consuls would be drawn in; exceptionally a gunboat would be sent. The Chinese government's prestige would suffer in the ensuing exchange of apologies and punishment of culprits. Meanwhile, the activity of the missionaries was steadily undermining the traditional society in more direct and didactic ways by preaching an individualism and egalitarianism alien to it and by acting as a magnet to converts to whom it offered economic and social advantages.

PEASANT REVOLTS

The process of undermining China also went forward directly by military and naval means; there were further impositions of concessions by force. But there was a growing ambiguity in the Chinese response. The authorities did not always resist the arrival of the foreigners. First the gentry of the areas immediately concerned and then the Peking (Beijing) government came round to feeling that foreign soldiers might not be without their value for the régime. Social disorder was growing. It could not be canalized solely against the foreigners and was threatening the establishment; China was beginning to undergo a cycle of peasant revolts which were to be the greatest in the whole of human history. In the middle decades of the century the familiar symptoms multiplied: banditry, secret societies. In the 1850s the "Red Turbans" were suppressed only at great cost. Such troubles frightened the establishment, and threw it on to the defensive, leaving it with little spare capacity to resist the steady gnawing of the West. These great rebellions were fundamentally caused by hunger for land and the most important and distinctive of them was the Taiping rebellion or, as it may more appropriately be called, revolution, which lasted from 1850 to 1864.

THE TAIPING REBELLION

THE HEART of this great convulsion, which cost the lives of more people than died the world over in the First World War, was a traditional peasant revolt. Hard times and a succession of natural disasters had helped to provoke it. It drew on a compound of land hunger, hatred of tax-gatherers, social envy and national resentment against the Manchus (though it is hard to see exactly what this

meant in practice, for most of the officials who actually administered the empire were, of course, themselves Chinese). It was also a regional outbreak, originating in the south and even there promoted by an isolated minority of settlers from the north. The new feature behind the revolt and one which made it ambiguous in the eyes of both Chinese and Europeans was that its leader, Hung Hsiu-ch'uan, had a superficial but impressive acquaintance with the Christian religion in the form of American Protestantism and this led him to denounce the worship of other gods, destroy idols – which included the Confucian ancestor tablets – and to talk of establishing the kingdom of God on earth. He had been rejected by his own culture, for he had been an unsuccessful candidate in the examinations which conferred status on low-born Chinese. Within the familiar framework of one of the periodic peasant upheavals of old China, that is to say, a new ideology was at work and showing itself subversive of the traditional culture and state. Some of its opponents at once grasped this and saw the Taiping movement as an ideological as well as a social challenge. Thus the revolution can be seen as an epoch in the Western disruption of China.

TAIPING IDEOLOGY

The Taiping army at first had a series of spectacular successes. By 1853 they had captured Nanking and established there the court of Hung Hsiu-ch'uan, now proclaimed the "Heavenly King". In spite of alarm further north, this was as far as they went. After 1856 the revolution was on the defensive. Nevertheless, it announced important social changes (which were to make it a source of inspiration for later Chinese reformers) and although it is by no means

The Heavenly Kingdom of the Taiping

The Taiping rebellion, inspired by its curious mixture of Chinese traditions and Protestant Christian influences, resulted in the bloodiest internal struggle in Chinese history.

The Taiping leader Hung Hsiu-ch'uan had convinced himself, through reading Christian texts and from visions he claimed to have had during an illness, that he was the younger brother of Christ and that his Father had charged him with the mission of liberating the Chinese people from the diabolical Manchu domination and showing them how to live in accordance with God's divine plan: the Great Peace. Hung Hsiu-ch'uan recruited a large army of discontented peasants, miners and charcoal workers from

the district of central Kwangsi. This army eventually took the important city of Nanking in 1853.

Although his followers executed homosexuals and prostitutes in the name of their leader's strict sexual morals, the "Heavenly King", once installed at Nanking, retired with his dozens of wives to a court made up exclusively of women. His officers soon began to fight among themselves. The movement's popularity waned: local people were alienated by its anti-Confucian stance; the poor Taiping followers felt let down by failure of the land redistribution scheme. In 1864, the imperial troops, armed with Western weapons and partly under the command of foreign generals, seized Nanking and quashed the rebellion.

This contemporary painting depicts the imperial Chinese troops launching their attack on the Taiping rebels at Tai. The rebels, outnumbered and ill-equipped, are shown beating a hasty retreat.

clear how widely these were effective or even appealing, their disruptive ideological effect was considerable. The basis of Taiping society was communism: there was no private property but communal provision for general needs. The land was in theory distributed for working in plots graded by quality to provide

just shares. Even more revolutionary was the extension of social and educational equality to women. The traditional binding of their feet was forbidden and a measure of sexual austerity marked the movement's aspirations (though not the conduct of the "Heavenly King" himself). These things reflected the mixture of religious and social elements which lay at the root of the Taiping cult and the danger it presented to the traditional order.

CHINESE CONCESSIONS TO EUROPEANS

The Taiping movement benefited at first from the demoralization brought about in the Manchu forces by their defeats at the hands of the Europeans and from the usual weaknesses shown by central government in China in a relatively distant and distinct region. As time passed and the Manchu forces were given abler (sometimes European) commanders, the bows and spears of the Taipings were proved insufficient. The foreigners, too, came to see the movement as a threat but kept up their pressure while the imperial government grappled with the Taipings. Treaties with France and the United States which followed that with Great Britain guaranteed the toleration of Christian missionaries and began the process of reserving jurisdiction over foreigners to consular and mixed courts. The danger presented by the Taiping revolution brought yet more concessions: new fighting resulted in the opening of more Chinese ports to foreign trade, the introduction to the Chinese customs administration of foreign superiors, the legalization of the sale of opium and the cession to the Russians of the province in which Vladivostok was to be built. It is hardly surprising that in 1861 the Chinese decided for the first time to set up a new department to deal with foreign affairs. The old myth that all the world recognized the Mandate of Heaven and owed tribute to the imperial court was dead.

In the end, the foreigners joined in against the Taipings. Whether their help was needed to end it is hard to say; certainly the Taiping movement was already failing. In 1864 Hung died and shortly afterwards Nanking fell to the Manchu. This was a victory for traditional China: the rule of the bureaucratic gentry had survived one more threat from below. None the less, an important turning-point had been reached. A rebellion had offered a revolutionary programme announcing a new danger, that the old challenge of peasant rebellion might be reinforced by an ideology from outside deeply corrosive to Confucian China. Nor did the end of the Taiping rebellion mean internal peace; from

This 1882 engraving depicts a Catholic missionary school in Peking. The image of Christ is surrounded by inscriptions in Chinese characters.

POTTIN.DEL.

Dated 1879, this engraving shows a Chinese market. Even in the latter part of the 19th century, there was still practically no Western presence in most of China.

the middle of the 1850s until well into the 1870s there were great Muslim risings in the northwest and southwest as well as other rebellions.

A KIND OF COLONIALISM

IMMEDIATELY AFTER THE SUPPRESSION of the Taiping rebellion, China showed even greater weakness in the face of the Western barbarians. Large areas had been devastated in the fighting; in many of them the soldiers were powerful and threatened the control of the bureaucracy. If the enormous loss of life did something to reduce pressure on land, this was probably balanced by a decline in the prestige and authority of the dynasty. Concessions had already had to be made to the Western powers under and because of these disadvantaged conditions; between 1856 and 1860 British and French forces were engaged every year against the Chinese. A treaty in 1861 brought to nineteen the number of "treaty ports" open to Western

merchants and provided for a permanent British ambassador at Peking. Meanwhile, the Russians exploited the Anglo-French successes to secure the opening of their entire border with China to trade. Further concessions would follow. It was evident that methods which had drawn the sting of nomadic invaders were not likely to work with confident Europeans whose ideological assurance and increasing technical superiority protected them from the seduction of Chinese civilization. When Roman Catholic missionaries were given the right to buy land and put up buildings Christianity was linked to economic penetration; soon the wish to protect converts meant involvement in the internal affairs of public order and police. It was impossible to contain the slow but continuous erosion of Chinese sovereignty. Never formally a colony, China was beginning none the less to undergo a measure of colonization.

Then there were territorial losses as the century wore on. In the 1870s the Russians seized the Ili valley (though they later handed much of it back) and in the next decade the French established a protectorate in Annam. Loosely asserted but ancient Chinese suzerainty was being swept away; the French began to absorb Indo-China and the British annexed Burma in 1886. The worst blow came from another Asiatic state; in the war of 1894–5 the Japanese took Formosa and the Pescadores, while China had to recognize the independence of Korea, from which they had received tribute since the seventeenth century. Following the Japanese success came further encroachments by other powers; provoked by the Russians, who established themselves in Port Arthur, England, France and Germany all extracted long leases of ports at the end of the century. Before this, the Portuguese, who had been in China longer than any other Europeans, converted their tenure of Macao into outright ownership. Even the Italians were in the market, though they did not actually get anything. And long before this, concessions, loans and agreements had been exacted by Western powers to protect and foster their own economic and financial interests. It is hardly surprising that when a British prime minister spoke at the end of the century of two classes of nation, the "living and the dying", China was regarded as an outstanding example of the second. Statesmen began to envisage her partition.

ATTEMPTS AT REFORM

Before the end of the nineteenth century it was evident to many Chinese intellectuals and civil servants that the traditional order would not generate the energy necessary to resist the new barbarians. Attempts along the old lines had failed. New tendencies began to appear. A "society for the study of self-strengthening" was founded to consider Western ideas and inventions which might be helpful. Its leaders cited the achievements of Peter the Great and, more significantly, those of contemporary reformers in Japan, an example all the more telling because of the superiority shown by the Japanese over China in war in 1895. Yet the would-be reformers still hoped that they would be able to root change in the Confucian tradition, albeit one purified and invigorated. They were members of the gentry and they succeeded in obtaining the ear of the emperor; they were thus working within the traditional framework and machinery of power to obtain administrative and technological reform without compromising the fundamentals of Chinese culture and ideology.

Unfortunately this meant that the Hundred Days of Reform of 1898 (as it came to be known) was almost at once tangled up in the court politics of the rivalry between the

emperor and the dowager empress, to say nothing of Chinese–Manchu antagonism. Though a stream of reform edicts was published, they were swiftly overtaken by a *coup d'état* by the empress, who locked up the emperor. The basic cause of the reformers' failure was the provocation offered by their inept political behaviour. Yet although the movement had failed, it was important that it had existed at all. It was to be a great stimulus to wider and deeper thinking about China's future.

A scene near the city wall in Peking is portrayed in this French engraving dated 1879.

THE BOXER MOVEMENT

For the moment, China seemed to have turned back to older methods of confronting the threat from outside, as a dramatic episode, the "Boxer movement", showed. Exploited by the empress, this was essentially a backward-looking and xenophobic upheaval which was given official diplomatic humiliation for China; an enormous indemnity was settled on customs henceforth under foreign direction.

SUN YAT-SEN

THE ENDING of the Boxer movement left China still more unstable. Reform had failed in 1898; so now had reaction. Perhaps only revolution lay ahead. Officers in the parts of the army which had undergone reorganization and training on Western lines began to think about it. Students in exile had already begun to meet and discuss their country's future, above all in Tokyo. The Japanese were happy to encourage subversive movements which might weaken their neighbour; in 1898 they had set up an "East Asian Cultural Union" from which emerged the slogan "Asia for the Asians". The Japanese

German sailors fight the Boxers, as depicted by an illustration in a contemporary French magazine.

encouragement. Missionaries and converts were murdered, a German minister killed and the foreign legations at Peking besieged, but the Boxers were unable to stand up to Western fighting-power. They once more revealed the hatred of foreigners which was waiting to be tapped, but also showed how little could be hoped for from the old structure, for its most conservative forces had dominated the movement, not the few reformers who became involved in it. It was suppressed by a military intervention which provides the only example in history of the armed forces of all the great powers operating under the same commander (a German, as it happened). The sequel was yet another

---

In defence of westernization

One of the defenders of the new reformist movement in China, which advocated the embracing of Western innovations, was the scholar Yen Fu (1854–1921), who translated the works of Adam Smith and John Stuart Mill. He wrote:

"There is not time to ask oneself if knowledge is Chinese or Western, or if it is new or old. If one path leads us to ignorance, and, therefore, to poverty and weakness, although it comes down from our ancestors or is based on the authority of our governors and masters ... we should leave it aside. If another path effectively conquers ignorance, and therefore frees us from our poverty and weakness, we should follow it although it comes from the barbarians ... ."

An extract from the writings of Yen Fu, 1900.

had great prestige in the eyes of the young Chinese radicals as Asians who were escaping from the trap of traditional backwardness which had been fatal to India and seemed to be about to engulf China. Japan could confront the West on terms of equality. Other students looked elsewhere for support, some to the long-enduring secret societies. One of them was a young man called Sun Yat-sen. His achievement has often been exaggerated, but, nevertheless, he attempted revolution ten times altogether. In the 1890s, he and others were asking only for a constitutional monarchy, but it was a very radical demand at that time.

Discontented exiles drew on support from Chinese businessmen abroad, of whom there were many, for the Chinese had always been great traders. They helped Sun Yat-sen to form in 1905 in Japan a revolutionary alliance aiming at the expulsion of the Manchus and the initiation of Chinese rule, a republican constitution, land reform. It sought to conciliate the foreigners, at this stage a wise tactical move, and the new programme showed the influence of Western thinkers (notably that of the English radical

A popular Chinese print from 1891 encourages the people to fight against foreign influences.

John Stuart Mill and the American economic reformer Henry George); once again the West provided the stimulus and some of the ideological baggage of a Chinese reform movement. This was the beginning of the party eventually to emerge as the dominant clique in the Chinese Republic.

Its formation, though, may well be thought less significant than another event of the same year, the abolition of the traditional examination system. More than any other institution, the examination system had continued to hold Chinese civilization together by providing the bureaucracy it recruited with its internal homogeneity and cohesion. These would not quickly wane, but the distinction between the mass of Chinese subjects and the privileged ruling class was now gone. Meanwhile, returning students from abroad, dissatisfied with what they found and no longer under the necessity of accommodating themselves to it by going through the examination procedure if they wished to enter government service, exercised a profoundly disturbing influence. They much increased the

In 1894 Sun Yat-sen (1866–1925), pictured here, founded the Association for the Regeneration of China, which was a revolutionary movement principally calling for national independence, agrarian reform and the formation of a republic.

The end of imperial China

Widespread discontent in early 20th-century China eventually allowed republican ideals (expressed by the growing group of young Chinese people who had been educated in the West) to triumph over the Manchu Dynasty. Revolution broke out almost by chance in 1911, when a group of officers took up arms after being implicated in the preparations for a revolution. A large number of cities rapidly joined the uprising and the defection of high-ranking army officers led to the collapse of the dynasty.

It was extremely difficult for republican democracy to take root in China – the country lacked not only the tradition of a representative government but also a public judiciary that was more than just a penal system. On Yuan Shih-kai's death in 1916 China would sink into unrest once more.

Yuan Shih-kai (1859–1916) was the second president of China, after Sun Yat-sen.

rate at which Chinese society began to be irradiated by Western ideas. Together with the soldiers in a modernized army, more and more of them looked to revolution for a way ahead.

THE CHINESE REPUBLIC

There were a number of rebellions (some directed by Sun Yat-sen from Indo-China with French connivance) before the empress and her puppet emperor died on successive days in 1908. The event raised new hopes but the Manchu government continued to drag its feet over reform. On the one hand it made important concessions of principle and promoted the flow of students abroad; on the other it showed that it could not achieve a decisive break with the past or surrender any of the imperial privileges of the Manchus. Perhaps more could not have been asked for. By 1911, the situation had deteriorated badly. The gentry class showed signs of losing its cohesion: it was no longer to back the dynasty in the face of subversion as it had done in the past. Governmentally, there existed a near-stalemate of internal power, the dynasty effectively controlling only a part of China. In October a revolutionary headquarters was discovered at Hankow. There had already been revolts which had been more or less contained earlier in the year. This precipitated one which at last turned into a successful revolution. Sun Yat-sen, whose name was used by the early rebels, was in the United States at the time and was taken by surprise.

The course of the revolution was decided by the defection from the régime of its military commanders. The most important of these was Yuan Shih-kai; when he turned on the Manchus, the dynasty was lost. The Mandate of Heaven had been withdrawn until on 12 February 1912 the last and six-year-old Manchu emperor abdicated. A republic had already been proclaimed, with Sun Yat-sen its president, and a new nationalist party soon appeared behind him. In March he resigned the presidency to Yuan Shih-kai; thus acknowledging where power really lay in the new republic and inaugurating a new phase of Chinese government, in which an ineffective constitutional régime at Peking disputed the practical government of China by warlords. This alone meant that China had still a long way to travel before she would be a modern nation-state. None the less, she had begun the half-century's march which would recover for her an independence lost in the nineteenth century to foreigners.

JAPAN

AT THE BEGINNING of the nineteenth century, there was little to show a superficial observer that Japan might adapt more successfully than China to challenges from the West. She was to all appearances deeply conservative. Yet much had already changed since the establishment of the shogunate and there were signs that the changes would cut deeper and faster as the years went by. One paradox is that this is in part attributable to the success of the Tokugawa era itself. It had brought peace. An obvious result was that Japan's military system became old-fashioned

and inefficient. The samurai themselves were evidently a parasitic class; warriors, there was nothing for them to do except to cluster in the castle-towns of their lords, consumers without employment, a social and economic problem. The prolonged peace also led to the surge of growth which was the most profound consequence of the Tokugawa era. Japan was already a semi-developed, diversifying society, with a money economy, the beginnings of a quasi-capitalist structure in agriculture which eroded the old feudal relationships, and a growing urban population.

A Japanese lady and her maid are portrayed in an 18th-century print. Thanks to the popularity at that time of such scenes from daily life, there is a wealth of graphic documentation on the Tokugawa era.

Osaka, the greatest mercantile centre, had between three and four hundred thousand inhabitants in the last years of the shogunate. Edo may have had a million. These great centres of consumption were sustained by financial and mercantile arrangements which had grown enormously in scale and complication since the seventeenth century. They made a mockery of the old notion of the inferiority of the merchant order. Even their techniques of salesmanship were modern; the eighteenth-century house of Mitsui (still today one of the great pillars of Japanese capitalism) gave free umbrellas decorated with their trade-mark to customers caught in their shops by the rain.

POLITICAL AND ECONOMIC INSTABILITY

Many of the changes that had taken place in Japan registered the creation of new wealth from which the shogunate had not itself bene-fited, largely because it was unable to tap it at a rate which kept pace with its own growing needs. The main revenue was the rice tax which flowed through the lords, and the rate at which the tax was levied remained fixed at the level of a seventeenth-century assessment. Taxation therefore did not take away the new wealth arising from better cultivation and land reclamation and, because this remained in the hands of the better-off peasants and village leaders, this led to sharpening contrasts in the countryside. The poorer peasantry was often driven to the labour markets of the towns. This was another sign of disintegration in the feudal society. In the towns, which suffered from an inflation made worse by the shogunate's debasement of the coinage, only the merchants seemed to prosper. A last effort of economic reform failed in the 1840s. The lords grew poorer and their retainers lost confidence; before the end of the Tokugawa, some samurai were beginning to dabble in trade. Their share of their lord's tax yield was still only that of their seventeenth-century predecessors; everywhere could be found impoverished, politically discontented swordsmen – and some aggrieved families of great lords who recalled the days when their race had stood on equal terms with the Tokugawa.

This print of a rice paddy is by Ando Hiroshige (1797–1858), who is known for his ability to evoke popular scenes. Japanese wood-cuts greatly influenced European painting at the end of the 19th century.

OPENNESS TO WESTERN INFLUENCES

The obvious danger of Japan's potential instability was all the greater because insulation against Western ideas had long since ceased to be complete. A few learned men had interested themselves in books which entered Japan through the narrow aperture of the Dutch trade. Japan was very different from China in its technical receptivity. "The Japanese are sharp-witted and quickly learn anything they see," said a sixteenth-century Dutchman. They had soon grasped and exploited as the Chinese never did the advantages of European firearms, and began to make them in quantity. They copied the European clocks, which the Chinese treated as toys. They were eager to learn from Europeans, as unhampered by their traditions as the Chinese seemed bogged down in theirs. On the great fiefs there were notable schools or research centres of "Dutch studies". The shogunate itself had authorized the translation of foreign books, an important step in so literate a society, for education in Tokugawa Japan had been almost too successful: even young samurai were beginning to enquire about Western ideas. The islands were relatively small and communications good, so that new ideas got about easily. Thus, Japan's posture when she suddenly had to face a new and unprecedented challenge from the West was less disadvantageous than that of China.

The first period of Western contact with Japan had ended in the seventeenth century, with the exclusion of all but a few Dutchmen allowed to conduct trade from an island at Nagasaki. Europeans had not then been able to challenge this outcome. That this was not likely to continue to be the case was shown in the 1840s by what happened to China, whose fate some of Japan's rulers observed with increasing alarm. The Europeans and North

Americans seemed to have both a new interest in breaking into Asian trade and new and irresistible strength to do it. The king of the Netherlands warned the shogun that exclusion was no longer a realistic policy. But there was no agreement among Japan's rulers about whether resistance or concession was the better. Finally, in 1851 the president of the United States commissioned a naval officer, Commodore Perry, to open relations with Japan. Under him, the first foreign squadron to sail into Japanese waters entered Edo Bay in 1853. In the following year it returned and the first of a series of treaties with foreign powers was made by the shogunate.

THE END OF THE SHOGUNATE

Perry's arrival could be seen in Confucian terms as an omen that the end of the shogunate was near. No doubt some Japanese saw it in that way. Yet this did not at once follow and there were a few years of somewhat muddled response to the barbarian threat. Japan's

The signing of a trade treaty between France and Japan is depicted in this engraving dated 1860.

rulers did not straightway come round to a wholehearted policy of concession (there was one further attempt to expel foreigners by force) and Japan's future course was not set until well into the 1860s. Within a few years the success of the West was none the less embodied in and symbolized by a series of so-called "unequal treaties". Commercial privileges, extra-territoriality for Western residents, the presence of diplomatic representatives and restrictions on the Japanese export of opium were the main concessions won by the United States, Great Britain, France, Russia and the Netherlands. Soon afterwards the shogunate came to an end; its inability to resist the foreigner was one contributing factor and another was the threat from two great aggregations of feudal power which had already begun to adopt Western military techniques in order to replace the Tokugawa by a more effective and centralized system under their control. There was fighting between the Tokugawa and their opponents, but it was followed not by a relapse into disorder and anarchy but by a resumption of power by the imperial court and administration in 1868 in the so-called "Meiji Restoration".

THE MEIJI RESTORATION

The re-emergence of the emperor and the widespread acceptance of the revolutionary renewal which followed was attributable above all to the passionate desire of most literate Japanese to escape from a "shameful inferiority" to the West which might have led them to share the fate of the Chinese and Indians. In the 1860s both the *bakufu* and some individual clans had already sent several missions to Europe. Anti-foreign agitation was dropped in order to learn from the West the secrets of its strength. There was a paradox in this. As in some European countries, a nationalism rooted in a conservative view of society was to dissolve much of the tradition it was developed to defend.

The transference of the court to Edo was the symbolic opening of the Meiji "Restoration" and the regeneration of Japan; its indispensable first stage was the abolition of feudalism. What might have been a difficult and bloody business was made simple by the voluntary surrender to the emperor of their lands by the four greatest clans, who set out their motives in a memorial they addressed to the emperor. They were returning to the emperor what had originally been his, they said, "so that a uniform rule may prevail throughout the empire. Thus the country will be able to rank equally with the other nations of the world." This was a concise expression of the patriotic ethic which was to inspire Japan's leaders for the next half-century and was widely spread in a country with a large degree of literacy where local leaders could make possible the acceptance of national goals to a degree impossible elsewhere. True, such expressions were not

This English engraving illustrates the opening of the Japanese parliament by the emperor on 29 November, 1890. It had been made clear to the members of the new legislature and to the Japanese public that the constitution of 1889 emanated from and could only be amended by the emperor's will.

uncommon in other countries. What was peculiar to Japan was the urgency which observation of the fate of China lent to the programme, the emotional support given to the idea by Japanese social and moral tradition, and the fact that in the imperial throne there was available within the established structure a source of moral authority not committed merely to maintaining the past. These conditions made possible a Japanese 1688: a conservative revolution opening the way to radical change.

JAPANESE "WESTERNIZATION"

Following the "Meiji Restoration", Japan rapidly adopted many of the institutions of Western government and Western society. A prefectorial system of administration, posts, a daily newspaper, a ministry of education, military conscription, the first railway, religious toleration and the Gregorian calendar all arrived within the first five years. A representative system of local government was inaugurated in 1879 and ten years later a new constitution set up a bicameral parliament (a peerage had already been created in preparation for the organization of the upper house). In fact, this was somewhat less revolutionary than it might appear, given the strong authoritarian strain in the document. At about the same time, too, the innovatory passion was beginning to show signs of flagging; the period when things Western were a craze was over; no such enthusiasm was to be seen again until the second half of the twentieth century. In 1890 an imperial Rescript on Education, subsequently to be read on great days to generations of Japanese schoolchildren, enjoined the observation of the traditional Confucian duties of filial piety and obedience and the sacrifice of self to the state if need be.

Japanese versus Western civilization

The conservative point of view on the contrast between the dynamics of Western culture and the immobility of Eastern culture is explained in this paragraph from a famous Japanese novel:

"Monarchy is not convenient, so parliamentary procedures are tried, which also disappoint and on to another thing. A river irritates, so a bridge is built; a mountain annoys, a tunnel is drilled. If communications are difficult, a railway line is built. But they never achieve total satisfaction. How far can man push forward his will in a positive way? Western civilization can be positive, progressive, but in the end it is a civilization created by people who are never satisfied. Japanese civilization does not look for satisfaction through changing things, but in man himself. Where this differs deeply from the West is in that it has been developed on the great assertion that it is not necessary to make fundamental changes in our surroundings. If relationships between parents and children are not the best, our civilization does not try to find harmony by changing those relationships, as the Europeans do. The relationships are thought to be unalterable and a means to restore serenity within them is sought."

An extract from *I Am A Cat* by Natsume Soseki (1906).

Much – perhaps the most important part – of old Japan was to survive the Meiji revolution and was to do so very obviously; this is in part the secret of modern Japan. But much, too, had gone. Feudalism could never be restored, generously compensated with government stock though the lords might be. Another striking expression of the new direction was the abolition of the old ordered class system. Care was shown in removing the privileges of the samurai; some of them could find compensation in the opportunities offered to them by the new bureaucracy, in business – no longer to be a demeaning activity – and in the modernized army and navy. For these foreign instruction was sought, because the Japanese sought proven excellence. Gradually they dropped their French military advisers and took to employing Germans after the Franco-Prussian War; the British provided instructors for the navy. Young Japanese were sent abroad to learn at first hand other secrets of the wonderful and threatening puissance of the West. It is still hard not to be moved by the ardour of many of these young men and of their elders and impossible not to be impressed by their achievement, which went far beyond Japan and their own time. The *shishi* (as some of the most passionate and dedicated activists of reform were called) later inspired national leaders right across Asia, from India to China. Their spirit was still at work in the young officers of the 1930s who were to launch the last and most destructive wave of Japanese imperialism.

ECONOMIC CHANGE

The crudest indexes of the success of the reformers are the economic, but they are very striking. They built on the economic benefits of the Tokugawa peace. It was not only the borrowing of Western technology and expertise which ensured the release in Japan of a current of growth achieved by no other non-Western state. The country was lucky in being already well-supplied with entrepreneurs who took for granted the profit motive and it was undoubtedly richer than, say, China. Some of the explanation of the great leap forward by Japan lay also in the overcoming of inflation and the liquidation of feudal restraints which had made it hard to tap Japan's full potential. The first sign of change was a further increase in agricultural production, little though the peasants, who made up four-fifths of the population in 1868, benefited from it. Japan managed to feed a growing population in the nineteenth century by bringing more land under cultivation for rice and by cultivating

This view of the Japanese city of Osaka was published in an English newspaper in 1891.

existing fields more intensively. Though the dependence on the land tax lessened as a bigger portion of the revenue could be found from other sources, it was still upon the peasant that the cost of the new Japan fell most heavily. As late as 1941, Japanese farmers saw few of the gains from modernization. Relatively they had fallen behind; their ancestors only a century earlier had a life expectancy and income approximating to that of their British equivalents, but even by 1900 this was far from true of their successors. There were few non-agricultural resources. It was the increasingly productive tax on land which paid for investment. Consumption remained low, though there was not the suffering of, say, the later industrialization process of Stalin's Russia. A high rate of saving (12 per cent in 1900) spared Japan dependence on foreign loans but, again, restricted consumption. This was the other side of the balance sheet of expansion whose credit entries were clear enough: the infrastructure of a modern state, an indigenous arms industry, a usually high credit rating in the eyes of foreign investors and a big expansion of cotton-spinning and other textiles by 1914.

SOCIAL UPHEAVAL

In the end a heavy spiritual cost had to be paid for these successes. Even while seeking to learn from the West, Japan turned inward. The "foreign" religious influences of Confucianism and even, at first, Buddhism, were attacked by the upholders of the state Shintoist cult, which, even under the shogunate, had begun to stress and enhance the role of the emperor as the embodiment of the divine. The demands of loyalty to the emperor as the focus of the nation came to override the principles embodied in the new

Prince Ito Hirobumi (1841–1909) headed the commission that prepared the Japanese constitution, travelling to Europe to study Western democratic models. He was a key figure in the westernization of Japan and held office as prime minister from 1886 intermittently until 1901.

constitution which might have been developed in liberal directions in a different cultural setting. The quality of the régime did not express itself in such institutions, but in the repressive actions of the imperial police. Yet it is difficult to see how an authoritarian emphasis could, in fact, have been avoided, given the two great tasks facing the statesmen of the Meiji Restoration. The modernization of the economy meant not planning in the modern sense but a strong governmental initiative and harsh fiscal policies. The other problem was order. The imperial power had once before gone into eclipse because of its failure to meet the threat on this front and now there were new dangers, because not all conservatives could be reconciled to the new model Japan. Discontented *ronin* – rootless samurai without masters – were one source of trouble. Another was peasant misery; there were scores of agrarian revolts in the first decade of the Meiji era. In the Satsuma rebellion of 1877 the government's new conscript

Japanese expansion 1895–1942

For half a century, Japan carried out an aggressive policy of military expansion. The wars with China (1894–1895) and Russia (1904–1905) allowed Japan to occupy Formosa and Korea. In 1931, the Japanese seized Manchuria from China; six years later they attacked China itself. In 1941, when Germany appeared to be winning the Second World War, Japan entered the war against the United States and Great Britain, in an attempt to impose Japanese rule over the whole of eastern Asia.

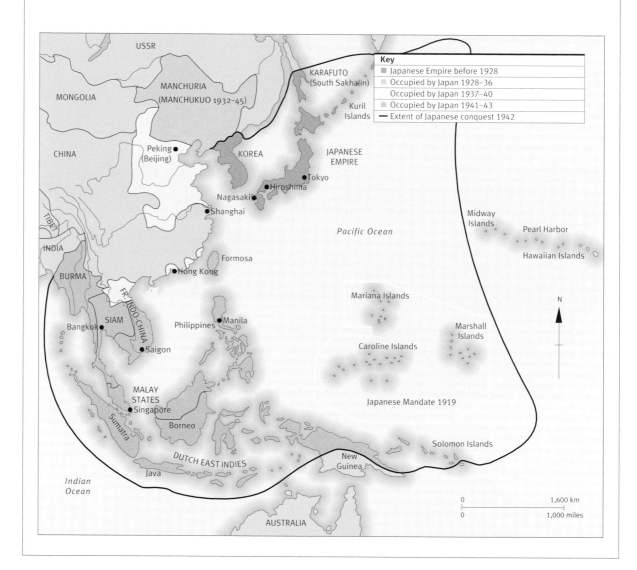

Key
- Japanese Empire before 1928
- Occupied by Japan 1928–36
- Occupied by Japan 1937–40
- Occupied by Japan 1941–43
- Extent of Japanese conquest 1942

forces showed that they could handle conservative resistance. It was the last of several rebellions against the Restoration and the last great challenge from conservatism.

The energies of the discontented samurai were gradually to be siphoned off into the service of the new state, but this did not mean that the implications for Japan were all beneficial. They intensified in certain key sectors of the national life an assertive nationalism which was to lead eventually to aggression abroad. Immediately, this was likely to find expression not only in resentment of the West but also in imperial ambitions directed towards the nearby Asian mainland. Modernization at home and adventure abroad were often in tension in Japan after the Meiji Restoration, but in the long run they pulled in the same direction. The popular and democratic movements especially felt the tug of imperialism.

RELATIONS WITH CHINA AND KOREA

China was the predestined victim of imperialist urges and was to be served as harshly by her fellow Asians as by any of the Western states. At first she was threatened only indirectly. Just as China's supremacy over the dependencies on her borders was challenged in Tibet, Indo-China and Manchuria by Europeans, so the Japanese threatened it in the ancient empire of Korea, long a tributary of Peking. Japanese interests there went back a long way. In part this was strategic; the Tsushima straits were the place where the mainland was nearest. In 1876 an overt move was made; under the threat of military and naval action which was very much like that used on China by the Europeans – and on Japan by Perry – the Koreans agreed to open three of their ports to the Japanese and to exchange diplomatic representation. Some Japanese already wanted more. They remembered earlier Japanese invasions and successful piracy on the Korean coast and pointed to the mineral and natural wealth of Korea. The statesmen of the Restoration did not at once give way to such pressure, but in a sense they were only making haste slowly. In the 1890s another step forward was taken which led Japan into her first major war since the Restoration, and it was against China. It was sweepingly successful but was followed by an appalling national humiliation, when in 1895 a group of Western powers forced Japan to accept a peace treaty much less advantageous than the one she had

imposed on the Chinese (which had included a declaration of Korea's independence).

WESTERN ACCEPTANCE OF JAPAN

At this point resentment of the West fused with enthusiasm for expansion in Asia. Popular dislike of the "unequal treaties" had been running high and the 1895 disappointment brought it to a head. The Japanese government had its own interests in backing Chinese revolutionary movements and now it had a slogan to offer them: "Asia for the Asians." It was becoming clear, too, to the Western powers that dealing with Japan was a very different matter from bullying China. Japan was increasingly recognized to be a "civilized" state, not to be treated like other non European nations. One symbol of the change was the ending in 1899 of one humiliating sign of European predominance, extra-territoriality. Then, in 1902, came the clearest acknowledgment of Japan's acceptance as an equal by the West,

This Japanese illustration of an episode in the war against China (1894–1895) emphasizes the overwhelming energy of the Japanese troops, whose modern uniforms contrast with the more traditional garb of the Chinese.

Japanese customs reach the West

From 1853, Western travellers were allowed to visit Japan for the first time in more than two centuries. The first Westerners to take advantage of this new openness were amazed to discover a highly refined Japanese culture. The mementos that visitors brought back with them made Japanese culture very fashionable in Europe in the latter part of the 19th century. European ladies took to wearing kimonos in private, and there was great interest in Japanese woodcuts, which inspired artists such as Van Gogh.

Some Japanese traditions were to become that country's identifying traits in the eyes of the rest of the world. These included the tea ceremony, with its detailed rituals and the beautiful, simplistic design of the objects used; Kabuki theatre; the elegance of the geishas; and the martial arts.

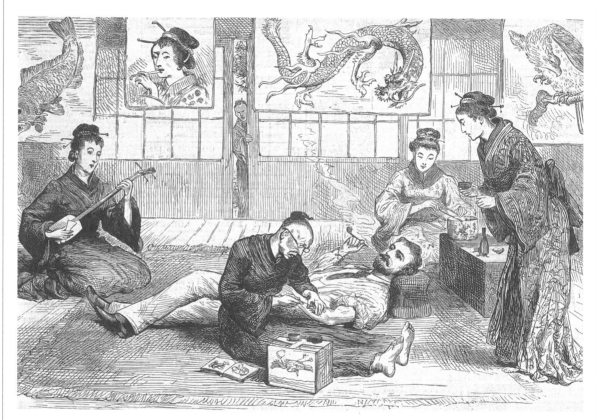

A European receives a tattoo in Nagasaki in 1882, attended by several geishas. Many Western visitors to 19th-century Japan were fascinated by the country's customs.

an Anglo-Japanese alliance. Japan, it was said, had joined Europe.

WAR WITH RUSSIA

At the beginning of the twentieth century Russia was the leading European power in the Far East. In 1895 her role had been decisive; her subsequent advance made it clear to the Japanese that the longed-for prize of Korea might elude them if they delayed. Railway-building, the development of Vladivostok, and Russian commercial activity in Korea – where politics was little more than the struggle of pro-Russian and pro-Japanese factions – were alarming. Most serious of all, the Russians had leased the naval base of Port Arthur from the enfeebled Chinese. In 1904 the Japanese struck. The result, after a year of war in Manchuria, was a humiliating defeat for the Russians. It was the end of tsarist pretensions in Korea and South Manchuria, where Japanese influence was henceforth dominant, and other territories passed into Japanese possession to remain there until 1945. But there was more to the Japanese victory than that. For the first time since the Middle Ages, non-Europeans had defeated a European power in a major war. The reverberations and repercussions were colossal.

A TURNING-POINT IN ASIA

The formal annexation of Korea by Japan in 1910, together with the Chinese Revolution of the following year and the end of Manchu rule, can now be seen as a milestone, the end of the first phase of Asia's response to the West, and as a turning-point. Asians had shown very differing reactions to Western

challenges. One of the two states which were to be the great Asian powers of the second half of the century was Japan, and she had inoculated herself against the threat from the West by accepting the virus of modernization. The other, China, had long striven not to do so.

In each case, the West provided both direct and indirect stimulus to upheaval, though in one case it was successfully contained and in the other it was not. In each case, too, the fate of the Asian power was shaped not only by its own response, but by the relations of the Western powers among themselves. Their rivalries had generated the scramble in China which had so alarmed and tempted the Japanese. The Anglo-Japanese alliance assured them that they could strike at their great enemy, Russia, and find her unsupported. A few years more and Japan and China would both be participants as formal equals with other powers in the First World War. Meanwhile, Japan's example and, above

The Japanese fleet is depicted in action against the Russians, off Port Arthur in Manchuria in 1904.

all, its victory over Russia, were an inspiration to other Asians, the greatest single reason for them to ponder whether European rule was bound to be their lot. In 1905 an American scholar could already speak of the Japanese as the "peers of Western peoples"; what they had done, by turning Europe's skills and ideas against her, might not other Asians do in their turn?

Everywhere in Asia European agencies launched or helped to launch changes which speeded up the crumbling of Europe's political hegemony. They had brought with them ideas about nationalism and humanitarianism, the Christian missionary's dislocation of local society and belief, and a new exploitation not sanctioned by tradition; all of which helped to ignite political, economic and social change. Primitive, almost blind, responses like the Indian Mutiny or the Boxer Rebellion were the first and obvious outcome, but there were others which had a much more important future ahead. In particular, this was true in India, the biggest and most important of all colonial territories.

This engraving dates from 1889 and depicts a visit to Bombay by the viceroy, Lord Lansdowne, who held office from 1888 to 1893.

COLONIAL INDIA

IN 1877 PARLIAMENT had bestowed the title of "Empress of India" upon Queen Victoria; some of her subjects laughed and a few disapproved, but it does not seem that there were many who did either. Most took the British supremacy there to be permanent or near-permanent and were not much concerned about names. They would have agreed with their compatriot who said "we are not in India to be pleasant" and held that only a severe and firm government could be sure to prevent another Mutiny. Others would also have agreed with the British viceroy who declared as the twentieth century began that: "As long as we rule India, we are the greatest power in the world. If we lose it, we shall drop straightaway to a third-rate power." Two important truths underlay this assertion. One was that the Indian taxpayer paid for the defence of much or most of the British Empire; Indian troops had been used to sustain it from Malta to China and in the subcontinent there was always a strategical reserve. The second was that Indian tariff policy was subordinated to British commercial and industrial realities.

IDEAS OF RACIAL SUPERIORITY

The economic and strategic importance of British India were the harsh facts whose weight was harder and harder to ignore. Yet they were not the whole story of the Raj. There was more to it than just fear, greed, cynicism or the love of power. Human beings do not find it easy to pursue collective purposes without some sort of myth to justify them; nor did the British in India. Some of them saw themselves as the heirs of the Romans whom a classical education taught them to admire, stoically bearing the burden of a lonely life in an alien land to bring peace to the warring and law to peoples without it. Others saw in Christianity a precious gift with which they must destroy idols and cleanse evil custom. Some never formulated such clear views but were simply convinced that what they brought was better than what they found and therefore what they were doing was good. At the basis of all these views there was a conviction of superiority and there was nothing surprising about this; it had always animated some imperialists. But in the later nineteenth century it was especially reinforced by fashionable racialist ideas and a muddled reflexion of what was thought to be taught by current biological science about the survival of the fittest. Such ideas provided another rationale for the much greater social separation of the British in India from native Indians after the shock of the Mutiny. Although there was a modest intake of nominated Indian landlords and native rulers into the legislative branch of government it was not until the very end of the century that these were joined by elected Indians. Moreover, though Indians could compete to enter the civil service, there were important practical obstacles in the way of their entry to the ranks of the decision-makers. In the army, too, Indians were kept

Imperial expansion in Southeast Asia (1850–1914)

Southeast Asia was divided between the main Western powers during the 19th century. The Dutch, who had settled in Java in the early 18th century, completed their domination of present-day Indonesia. The British established their rule over Burma, Malaya and the northern part of Borneo, while the French took over Indo-China. In 1899, the United States replaced Spain as a colonial power in the Philippines. Uniquely, the kingdom of Siam (now Thailand) maintained its independence.

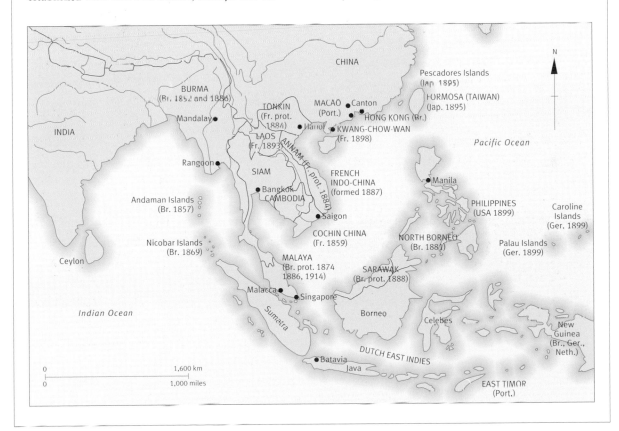

Painted in the Moghul tradition, this 19th-century portrait represents the Indian maharaja Gulab Singh. Having signed a treaty with the British at the end of the Sikh War in 1846, Singh became ruler of the combined states of Jammu and Kashmir in northwestern India. Kashmir, a region rich in wildlife, became popular with British hunters.

out of the senior commissioned ranks.

The largest single part of the British army was always stationed in India, where its reliability and monopoly of artillery combined with the officering of the Indian regiments by Europeans to ensure that there would be no repetition of the Mutiny. The coming of railways, telegraphs and more advanced weapons in any case told in favour of government in India as much as in any European country. But armed force was not the explanation of the self-assuredness of British rule, any more than was a conviction of racial superiority. The Census Report of 1901 recorded that there were just under three hundred million Indians. These were governed by about 900 white civil servants. Usually there was about one British soldier for every four thousand Indians. As an Englishman once put it, picturesquely, had all the Indians chosen to spit at the same moment, his countrymen would have been drowned.

THE ADMINISTRATION OF THE RAJ

THE RAJ RESTED on carefully administered policies. One assumption underlying them after the Mutiny was that Indian society should be interfered with as little as possible. Female infanticide, since it was murder, was forbidden, but there was to be no attempt to prohibit polygamy or child marriage (though after 1891 it was not legal for a marriage to be consummated until the wife was twelve years old). The line of the law was to run outside what was sanctioned by Hindu religion. This conservatism was reflected in a new attitude towards the native Indian rulers. The Mutiny had shown that they were usually loyal; those who turned against the government had been provoked by resentment against British annexation of their lands. Their rights were therefore scrupulously respected after the Mutiny; the princes ruled their own states independently and virtually irresponsibly, checked only by their awe of the British political officers resident at their courts. The native states included over a fifth of the population. Elsewhere, the British cultivated the native aristocracy and the landlords. This was part of a search for support from key groups of Indians, but often led the British to lean on those whose own leadership powers were already being undermined by social change. Enlightened despotism at their expense, but in the interests of the peasantry (such as had been shown earlier in the century) none the less now disappeared. These were all some of the unhappy consequences of the Mutiny.

A RISING TIDE OF DISCONTENT

No more than any other imperial government was the Raj able permanently to ensure itself against change. Its very success told against it. The suppression of warfare favoured the growth of population – and one consequence was more frequent famine. But the provision of ways of earning a living other than by agriculture (which was a possible outlet from the problem of an overpopulated countryside) was made very difficult by the obstacles in the way of Indian industrialization. These arose in large measure from a tariff policy in the interest of British manufactures. A slowly emerging class of Indian industrialists did not, therefore, feel warmly towards govern-

The British army in India is shown during training exercises in 1891. This army was the ultimate defence of the security of India from the time of the failed Mutiny until Indian independence.

R. Caton Woodville

ment, but were antagonized by it. Their ranks also included many of the growing number of Indians who had received an education along English lines and had subsequently been irritated to compare its precepts with the practice of the British community in India. Some who had gone to England to study at Oxford, Cambridge or the Inns of Court found the contrast especially galling: in England there were even Indian Members of Parliament in the nineteenth century, while an Indian graduate in India might be slighted by a British private soldier, and there was an outcry from British residents when, in the 1880s, a viceroy wished to remove the "invidious distinction" which prevented a European from being brought before an Indian magistrate. Some, too, had pondered what they read in their studies; John Stuart Mill and Mazzini were thus to have a huge influence in India, and, through its leaders, in the rest of Asia.

THE HINDU NATIONALIST MOVEMENT

Resentment was especially felt among the Hindus of Bengal, the historic centre of British power: Calcutta was the capital of India. In 1905 this province was divided in two. This partition was an important landmark, for it for the first time brought the Raj into serious conflict with something which had not existed in 1857, the Indian nationalist movement.

At every stage this movement had been fed and stimulated by non-Indian forces. British orientalists, at the beginning of the nineteenth century, had begun the rediscovery of classical Indian culture which was essential both to the self-respect of Hindu nationalism and the overcoming of the subcontinent's huge divisions. Indian scholars began to bring to light, under European guidance, the culture and religion embedded in the neglected Sanskrit scriptures; through these they could formulate a conception of a Hinduism far removed from the rich and fantastic, but also superstitious, accretions of its popular form. By the end of the nineteenth century this recovery of the Aryan and Vedic past – Islamic India was virtually disregarded – had gone far enough for Hindus to meet with confidence the reproaches of Christian missionaries and offer a cultural counter-attack; a Hindu emissary to a "Parliament of Religions" in Chicago in 1893 not only awoke great personal esteem and obtained

Food is handed out in India during a drought, in a drawing published by an Italian newspaper in 1902. The huge population growth that occurred in India under British rule played its part in making famine more frequent and serious.

serious attention for his assertion that Hinduism was a great religion capable of revivifying the spiritual life of other cultures, but actually made converts.

The Hindu national consciousness, like the political activity it was to reinforce, was for a long time confined to a few. The proposal that Hindi should be India's language seemed wildly unrealistic when the hundreds of languages and dialects which fragmented Indian society were considered and could only appeal to an élite seeking to strengthen its links across a subcontinent. The definition of its membership was education rather than wealth: its backbone was provided by those Hindus, often Bengali, who felt especially disappointed at the failure of their educational attainments to win them an appropriate share in the running of India. The Raj seemed determined to maintain the racial predominance of Europeans and to rely upon such conservative interests as the princes and landlords, to the exclusion and, possibly even more important, the humiliation of the *babu*, the educated, middle-class, urban Hindu.

THE INDIAN NATIONAL CONGRESS

A new cultural self-respect and a growing sense of grievance over rewards and slights were the background to the formation of the Indian National Congress. The immediate prelude was a flurry of excitement over government proposals, subsequently modified because of the outcry of European residents, to equalize the treatment of Indians and Europeans in the courts. Disappointment caused an Englishman, a former civil servant, to take the steps which led to the first conference of the Indian National Congress in Bombay in December 1885. Vice-regal initiatives, too, had played a part in this, and Europeans were long to be prominent in the

> ### The strength of the Hindu faith
>
> A French traveller who visited India in 1864 to 1868 was amazed by the great religious tolerance the Hindus showed:
>
> "In what country can one contemplate the spectacle offered before our eyes that day in the square in Benares [Varanasi]. Ten paces from all that the Indian holds most sacred in his religion, between the fountain of Wisdom and the idol of Shiva, under a tree, a Protestant missionary stood on a chair, and preached in native languages about the Christian religion and the errors of paganism. I heard his screeching voice when he said to the crowd, who stood round him respectfully, 'You are idolatrizers! That stone you worship was chiselled out of a quarry and is as inert, as impotent as the post on the corner of my street.' These words did not cause even a murmur; they listened impassively to the missionary, but they were following his speech because now and again one of them asked a question, which the evangelist tried to answer as best he could. Perhaps the missionary's courage would be more admirable if the Indians' tolerance were not so well known. One of them said to me one day, 'Our work is useless, because one can never convert a man who is so confident of his own faith that he can listen to our attacks against it without becoming upset.'"
>
> An extract from *Rajas' Travels in India* by Louis Rousselet.

administration of Congress. Even longer would they patronize it with protection and advice in London. It was an appropriate symbol of the complexity of the European impact on India that some Indian delegates attended in European dress, improbably attired in morning-suits and top-hats of comical unsuitability to the climate of their country, but the formal attire of its rulers.

Congress was soon committed by its declaration of principles to national unity and regeneration: as in Japan already and China

The Indian National Congress

The organization that was to lead India to independence in 1947, and which would govern as the leading party for the first decades of independence, was established in Bombay in December 1885. The 70 delegates who founded the Indian National Congress did not contest British rule. However, in the years that followed, Indian nationalist feelings grew and Congress (although it was always careful to stay within the law) became a voice of opposition to British politics in India.

At the beginning of the 20th century, the increasing tension between Hindus and Muslims considerably complicated the Indian political situation. Although extreme nationalists opted for the use of terrorism, Congress long remained loyal to Great Britain.

Founder members of the Indian National Congress are portrayed in this 19th-century photograph.

and many other countries later, this was the classical product of the impact of European ideas. But it did not at first aspire to self-government. Congress sought, rather, to provide a means of communicating Indian views to the viceroy and proclaimed its "unswerving loyalty" to the British Crown. Only after twenty years, in which much more extreme nationalist views had won adherents among Hindus, did it begin to discuss the possibility of independence. During this time its attitude had been soured and stiffened by the vilification it received from British residents who declared it unrepresentative, and the unresponsiveness of an administration which endorsed this view and preferred to work through more traditional and conservative social forces. Extremists became more insistent. In 1904 came the inspiring victories of Japan over Russia. The issue for a clash was provided in 1905 by the administrative division of Bengal.

THE PARTITION OF BENGAL

The purpose of the partition was twofold: it was administratively convenient and it would possibly weaken Bengal's nationalism. It produced a West Bengal where there was a Hindu majority, and an East Bengal with a Muslim majority. This detonated a mass of explosive materials long accumulating. Immediately, there was a struggle for power in Congress. At first a split was avoided by agreement on the aim of *swaraj*, which in practice might mean independent self-government such as that enjoyed by the white dominions: their example was suggestive. The extremists were heartened by anti-partition riots. A new weapon was deployed against the British, a boycott of goods, which, it was hoped, might be extended to other forms of passive resistance such as non-payment of taxes and the refusal of soldiers to obey orders. By 1908 the extremists were excluded from Congress. By this time, a second consequence was apparent: extremism was producing terrorism. Again, foreign models were important. Russian revolutionary terrorism now joined the works of Mazzini and the biography of Garibaldi, the guerrilla leader hero of Italian independence, as formative influences on an emerging India. The extremists argued that political murder was not ordinary murder. Assassination and bombing were met with special repressive measures.

The third consequence of partition was perhaps the most momentous. It brought out into the open the division of Muslim and Hindu.

MUSLIMS AND HINDUS

For reasons which went back to the percolation of Muslim India before the Mutiny by an Islamic reform movement, the Arabian Wahhabi sect, Indian Muslims had for a century felt themselves more and more distinct from Hindus. Distrusted by the British because of attempts to revivify the Moghul Empire in 1857, they had little success in winning posts in government or on the judicial bench. Hindus had responded more eagerly than Muslims to the educational opportunities offered by the Raj; they were of more commercial weight and had more influence on government. But Muslims too, had found their British helpers, who had established a new, Islamic college, providing the English education they needed to compete with Hindus, and had helped to set up Muslim political organizations. Some English civil servants began to grasp the potential for balancing Hindu pressure which this could give the Raj. Intensification of Hindu ritual practice such as a cow protection movement was not likely to do anything but increase the separation of the two communities.

Nevertheless, it was only in 1905 that the split became, as it remained, one of the fundamentals of the subcontinent's politics. The anti-partitionists campaigned with a strident display of Hindu symbols and slogans. The British governor of eastern Bengal favoured Muslims against Hindus and strove to give them a vested interest in the new province. He was dismissed, but his inoculation had taken: Bengal Muslims deplored his removal. An Anglo-Muslim entente was in the making. This further inflamed Hindu terrorists. To make things worse, all this was taking place during five years (from 1906 to 1910) in which prices rose faster than at any time since the Mutiny.

COMMUNAL POLITICS

An important set of political reforms conceded in 1909 did not do more than change somewhat the forms with which to operate the political forces which were henceforth to dominate the history of India until

A temple to the Hindu goddess Kali in Calcutta is depicted in this illustration dated 1887. Worshippers of the goddess could descend the temple steps to bathe in the purifying waters of the River Hooghly, one of the tributaries of the Ganges delta.

the Raj came to an end nearly forty years later. Indians were for the first time appointed to the council which advised the British minister responsible for India and, more important, further elected places were provided for Indians in the legislative councils. But the elections were to be made by electorates which had a communal basis; the division of Hindu and Muslim India, that is to say, was institutionalized.

In 1911, for the first and only time, a reigning British monarch visited India. A great imperial durbar was held at Delhi, the old centre of Moghul rule, to which the capital of British India was now transferred from Calcutta. The princes of India came to do homage; Congress did not question its duty to the throne. The accession to the throne of George V that year had been marked by the conferring of real and symbolic benefits, of which the most notable and politically significant was the reuniting of

Bengal. If there was a moment at which the Raj was at its apogee, this was it.

MUSLIM DISCONTENT

Yet India was far from settled. Terrorism and seditious crime continued. The policy of favouring the Muslims had made Hindus more resentful while Muslims now felt that the government had gone back on its understandings with them in withdrawing the partition of Bengal. They feared the resumption of a Hindu ascendancy in the province. Hindus, on the other hand, took the concession as evidence that resistance had paid and began to press for the abolition of the communal electoral arrangements which the Muslims prized. The British had therefore done much to alienate Muslim support when a further strain appeared. The Indian Muslim élites which had favoured cooperation with the British were increasingly under pressure from more middle-class Muslims susceptible to the violent appeal of a pan-Islamic movement. The pan-Islamists could point to the fact that the British had let the Muslims down in Bengal, but also noted that in Tripoli (which the Italians attacked in 1911) and the Balkans in 1912 and 1913, Christian powers were attacking Turkey, the seat of the Caliphate, the institutional embodiment of the spiritual leadership of Islam, and Great Britain was, indisputably, a Christian power. The intense susceptibilities of lower-class Indian Muslims were excited to the point at which even the involvement of a mosque in the replanning of a street could be presented as a part of a deliberate plot to harry Islam. When in 1914 Turkey decided to go to war with Great Britain, though the Muslim League remained loyal, some Indian Muslims accepted the logical consequence of the Caliphate's supremacy, and began to prepare revolution against the Raj. They were few. What was more important for the future was that by that year not two but three forces were making the running in Indian politics, the British, Hindu and Muslim. Here was the origin of the future partition of the only complete political unity the subcontinent had ever known, and, like that unity, it was as much the result of the play of non-Indian as of Indian forces.

SOUTHEAST ASIA

INDIA WAS THE LARGEST single mass of non-European population and territory under European rule in Asia, but to the south-east and in Indonesia, both part of the Indian cultural sphere, lay further imperial possessions. Few generalizations are possible about so huge an area and so many peoples and religions. One negative fact was observable: in

no other European possession in Asia was there such transformation before 1914 as in India, though in all of them modernization had begun the corrosion of local tradition. The forces which produced this were those which have already been noted at work elsewhere: European aggression, the example of Japan, and the diffusion of European culture.

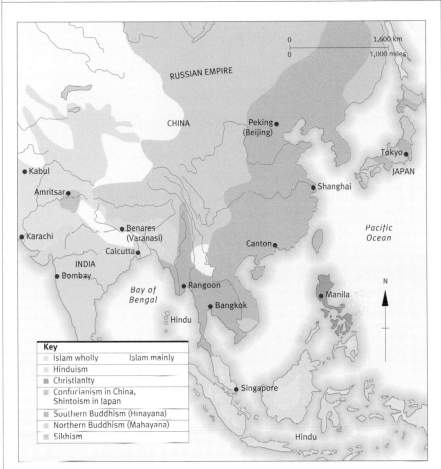

The major religions of Asia in the early 20th century

The religious composition of Asia in the early 20th century was the result of thousands of years of history. Hinduism, which predominates in India, has inherited a tradition which is more than 3,000 years old. Islam entered India in the 11th century and Indonesia in the 13th century. The Buddha's preaching in India 2,500 years ago gave rise to two branches of Buddhism, one of which spread through Tibet, China, Korea and Japan, and the other through Ceylon and Indo-China. In China and Japan the ancient traditions of Confucianism and Shintoism, respectively, survived the influx of new creeds. In the 15th century, Sikhism was founded by Guru Nanak and began to take root in the Indian region of the Punjab. Finally Christianity reached the Philippines in the 16th century.

But the first and last of these forces operated in the region for a shorter time before 1914 than in China and India. In 1880 most of mainland Southeast Asia was still ruled by native princes who were independent rulers, even if they had to make concessions in "unequal treaties" to European power. In the following decade this was rapidly changed by the British annexation of Burma and continuing French expansion in Indo-China. The sultans of Malaya acquired British residents at their courts who directed policy through the native administration, while the "Straits settlements" were ruled directly as a colony. By 1900 only Siam was still independent among the kingdoms of this region.

FRENCH INDO-CHINA

Most Southeast Asian kingdoms had been shaped by cultural influences which were Indian in origin. The only one which was culturally more closely linked to China was Vietnam, that part of Indo-China known in the early stages of French Asian expansion as Annam. Vietnam had the longest tradition of

Indian troops cross a river after having fought rebel tribes in Manipur, near the Burmese frontier. Upper Burma was integrated into the British Empire in 1886.

national identity and a history of national revolt long before the European imperial era. It is not therefore surprising to find that it was here that Indo-Chinese resistance to Europeanization was most marked.

French interest in the area went back to Christian missions in the seventeenth century. In the 1850s the persecution of Christianity led the French (briefly assisted by the Spanish) to intervene in South Vietnam, then known as Cochin China. This brought about diplomatic conflict with China, which claimed sovereignty over the country. In 1863 the emperor of Annam ceded part of Cochin China under duress to the French and Cambodia accepted a French protectorate. This was followed by further French advance and the arousing of Indo-Chinese resistance. In the 1870s the French occupied the Red River delta; soon, other quarrels led to a war with China, the paramount power, which confirmed the French grip on Indo-China. In 1887 they set up an Indo-Chinese Union which disguised a centralized régime behind a system of protectorates. Though this meant the preservation of native rulers (the emperor of Annam and the kings of Cambodia and Laos), the aim of French colonial policy was always assimilation. French culture was to be brought to new French subjects whose élites were to be gallicized because this was believed to be the best way to modernization and civilization.

OPPOSITION TO FRENCH RULE

The centralizing tendencies of French administration soon made it clear that the formal structure of native government was a sham. Unwittingly, the French thus sapped local institutions without replacing them with others enjoying the loyalty of the people. This was a dangerous course. There were also

Of European origin, this 19th-century engraving shows Christians being beheaded in Cochin China.

other important by-products of the French presence. It brought with it, for example, French tariff policy, which was to slow down industrialization. This eventually led Indo Chinese businessmen, like their Indian equivalents, to wonder in whose interests their country was run. Moreover, the conception of an Indo-China which was integrally a part of France, whose inhabitants should be turned into French citizens, also brought problems. The French administration had to grapple with the paradox that access to French education could lead to reflexion on the inspiring motto to be found on official buildings and documents of the Third Republic: "liberty, equality and fraternity." Finally, French law and notions of property broke down the structure of village land-holding and threw power into the hands of money-lenders and landlords. With a growing population in the rice-growing areas, this

was to build up a revolutionary potential for the future.

Japan and China provided catalysts for Indo-Chinese grievances embodied in these facts and the legacy of traditional Vietnamese nationalism soon made itself felt. The Japanese victory over Russia led several young Vietnamese to go to Tokyo, where they met Sun Yat-sen and the Japanese sponsors of "Asia for the Asians". After the Chinese Revolution of 1911, one of them organized a society for a Vietnamese Republic. None of this much troubled the French who were well able to contain such opposition before 1914, but it curiously paralleled conservative opposition to them among the Vietnamese Confucian scholar class. Though they opened a university in 1907, the French had to close it almost at once and it remained closed until 1918 because of fears of unrest among the intellectuals. This important section of

In the kingdom of Tonkin, which was part of French Indo-China, the regional colonial commander receives local petitioners in front of his residence in the early 1900s.

Vietnamese opinion was already deeply alienated by French rule within a couple of decades of its establishment.

INDONESIA

To THE SOUTH of Indo-China, too, French history had already had an indirect impact in Indonesia. By the end of the nineteenth century there were some sixty million Indonesians; population pressure had not yet produced there the strains that were to come, but it was the largest group of non-Europeans ruled by a European state outside India. Their ancestors had nearly two centuries of sometimes bitter experience of Dutch rule before the French Revolution led to the invasion of the United Provinces, the setting up of a new revolutionary republic there in 1795 and the dissolving of the Dutch East India Company. Equally important, there soon followed a British occupation of Java. The British troubled the waters by important changes in the revenue system, but there were also other influences now at work to stir up Indonesia. Though originally an outcropping of the Hindu civilization of India, it was also part of the Islamic world, with large numbers of at least nominal Muslims among its peoples, and commercial ties with Arabia. In the early years of the nineteenth century this had new importance. Indonesian pilgrims, some of them of birth and rank, went to Mecca and then sometimes went on to Egypt and Turkey. There they found themselves directly in touch with reforming ideas from further west.

ANTI-DUTCH FEELING

The instability of the situation in Indonesia was revealed when the Dutch returned and had, in 1825, to fight a "Java War" against a dissident prince which lasted five years. It damaged the island's finances so that the Dutch were constrained to introduce further changes. The result was an agricultural system which enforced the cultivation of crops for the government. The workings of this system led to grave exploitation of the peasant which began in the later nineteenth century to awaken among the Dutch an uneasiness about the conduct of their colonial government. This culminated in a great change of attitude; in 1901 a new "Ethical Policy" was announced which was expressed in decentralization and a campaign to achieve improvement through village administration. But this programme often proved so paternalistic and interventionist in action that it, too, sometimes stimulated hostility. This was utilized by the first Indonesian nationalists, some of them inspired by Indians. In 1908 they formed an organization to promote national education. Three years later an Islamic association appeared whose early activities were directed as much against Chinese traders as against the Dutch. By 1916 it had gone so far as to ask for self-government while remaining in union with the Netherlands. Before this, however, a true independence party had been founded in 1912. It opposed Dutch authority in the name of native-born Indonesians, of any race; a Dutchman was among its three founders and others followed him. In 1916 the Dutch took the first step towards meeting the demands of these groups by authorizing a parliament with limited powers for Indonesia.

THE LEGACY OF IMPERIALISM IN ASIA

Though European ideas of nationalism were by the early years of the twentieth century at work in almost all Asian countries, they took

The European influence is unmistakable in this illustration of a street in Java in 1886.

their different expressions from different possibilities. Not all colonial régimes behaved in the same way. The British encouraged nationalists in Burma, while the Americans doggedly pursued a benevolent paternalism in the Philippines after suppressing insurrection originally directed against their Spanish predecessors. Those same Spanish, like the Portuguese elsewhere in Asia, had vigorously promoted Christian conversion, while the British Raj was very cautious about interference with the native religions. History also shaped the futures of colonial Asia, because of the different legacies different European régimes played there. Above all, the forces of historical possibilities and historical inertia showed themselves in Japan and China, where direct European influence was just as dramatic in its effects as in India or Vietnam. In every instance, the context in which that influence operated was decisive in shaping the future; at the end of a couple of centuries of European activity in Asia much (perhaps most) of that context remained intact. A huge residue of customary thought and practice remained undisturbed. Too much history was present for European expansion alone to explain twentieth-century Asia. The catalytic and liberating power of that expansion, none the less, brought Asia into the modern era.

Albert Sarraut, the governor of French Indo-China, poses with Emperor Khai Dai of Annam. Khai Dai's son Bao Dai (who was born in 1913) ruled as the last emperor of Annam from 1932 until 1945, when he was deposed and the Republic of Vietnam was declared.

4 STRAINS IN THE SYSTEM

Early incubators are used to care for babies in a Parisian maternity hospital in 1884. Premature babies were laid in wooden structures which were then placed over metal containers full of hot water to keep the infants at the correct temperature. The use of incubators contributed to the drop in the infant mortality rate in Europe in the late 19th and early 20th centuries.

ONE HISTORICAL TREND very obvious as the twentieth century opened was the continuing increase of population in the European world. In 1900 Europe had about four hundred million inhabitants – a quarter of them Russians – the United States about seventy-six million and the British overseas dominions about 15 million between them. This kept the dominant civilization's share of world population high. On the other hand, growth was already beginning to slow down in some countries in the first decade of this century. This was most obvious in the advanced nations which were the heart of Western Europe, where growth depended

more and more on falling death-rates. In them there was evidence that keeping your family small was a practice now spreading downwards through society. Traditional contraceptive knowledge of a sort had long been available, but the nineteenth century had brought to the better-off more effective techniques. When these were taken up more widely (and there were soon signs that they were), their impact on population structure would be very great.

FEARS OF WORLD OVERPOPULATION

In Eastern and Mediterranean Europe, on the other hand, major changes in the population structure were far away. There, rapid growth was only just beginning to produce grave strains. The growing availability of outlets though emigration in the nineteenth century had made it possible to overcome them; there might be trouble to come if those outlets ceased to be so easily available. Further afield, even more pessimistic reflexions might be prompted by considering what would happen when the agencies at work to reduce the death-rate in Europe came to spread to Asia and Africa. In the world civilization the

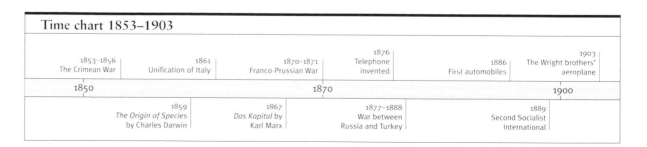

Time chart 1853–1903					
1853–1856 The Crimean War	1861 Unification of Italy	1870–1871 Franco-Prussian War	1876 Telephone invented	1886 First automobiles	1903 The Wright brothers' aeroplane
1850		1870			1900
	1859 *The Origin of Species* by Charles Darwin	1867 *Das Kapital* by Karl Marx	1877–1888 War between Russia and Turkey	1889 Second Socialist International	

nineteenth century had created, this could not be prevented. In that case, Europe's success in imposing itself would have guaranteed the eventual loss of the demographic advantage recently added to her technical superiority. Worst still, the Malthusian crisis once feared (but lost to sight as the nineteenth-century economic miracle removed the fear of over-population) might at last become a reality.

RAPID ECONOMIC GROWTH

It had been possible to set aside Malthus' warnings because the nineteenth century brought about the greatest expansion of wealth the world had ever known. Its sources lay in the industrialization of Europe, and the techniques for assuring the continuance of this growth were by no means exhausted or compromised in 1900. There had not only been a vast and accelerating flow of com-modities available only in (relatively) tiny quantities a century before, but whole new ranges of goods had come into existence. Oil and electricity had joined coal, wood, wind and water as sources of energy. A chemical industry existed which could not have been envisaged in 1800. Growing power and wealth had been used to tap seemingly inex-haustible natural resources, both agricultural and mineral. Railways, electric trams, steamships, motor cars and bicycles gave to millions a new control over their environ-ment; they quickened travel from place to place and eased transport for the first time since animals had been harnessed to carts thousands of years before. The overall result of such changes had been that in many coun-tries a growing population had been easily carried on an even faster growing production of wealth; between 1870 and 1900, for exam-ple, Germany's output of pig-iron increased sixfold, but her population rose only by

Migration from Europe in the 19th century

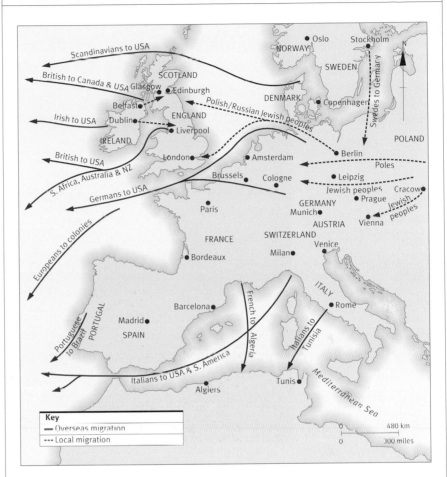

During the 19th century, the main population movement was that of the Europeans emigrating to America. The sparsely populated territories of the United States, and to a lesser extent South American countries such as Argentina and Brazil, offered wonder-ful opportunities to immigrants. Many Japanese and Chinese people also emigrated to America. The colonies seemed less attractive to European settlers, although there were some exceptions, including Australia.

Within Europe itself, the main population movement was that of the Jews, who left the hostile tsarist Russian Empire in large numbers to settle in the Western European states.

about a third. In terms of consumption, or of the services to which they had access, or in the enjoyment of better health, even the mass of the population in developed countries were much better off in 1900 than their predeces-sors a hundred years before. This still left out people like the Russian or Andalusian peas-ants (though an assessment of their condition is by no means easy to make nor the result a

This painting, entitled *The Forge*, dates from 1893. At that time, the iron and steel industries were enormously important in Europe: economic and military power could not be achieved without them.

foregone conclusion). But, none the less, the way ahead looked promising even for them, inasmuch as a key to prosperity had been found which could be made available to all countries.

POVERTY IN INDUSTRIAL EUROPE

In spite of the cheerful picture presented by growing prosperity, doubts could break in. Even if what might happen in the future were ignored, contemplation of the cost of the new wealth and doubts about the social justice of its distribution were troubling. Most people were still terribly poor, whether or not they lived in rich countries where the incongruity of this was more striking than in earlier times.

Poverty was all the more afflicting when society showed such obvious power to create new wealth. Here was the beginning of a change of revolutionary import in expectations. Another change in the way Europeans thought about their condition arose over their power to get a livelihood at all. It was not new that wage-earners should be without work. What was new was that situations should suddenly arise in which the operation of blind forces of boom and slump produced millions of men without work concentrated in great towns. This was "unemployment", the new phenomenon for which a new word had been needed. Some economists thought that it might be an inevitable concomitant of capitalism. Nor were the cities themselves yet rid of all the evils which had so struck the first observers of industrial society. By 1900

the majority of Western Europeans were town-dwellers. By 1914 there were more than 140 cities of over a hundred thousand inhabitants. In some of them, millions of people were cramped, ill-housed, underprovided with schools and fresh air, let alone amusement other than that of the streets, and this often in sight of the wealth their society helped to produce. "Slums" was another word invented by the nineteenth century. Two converging conclusions were often drawn from contemplating them. One was that of fear; many sober statesmen at the end of the nineteenth century still distrusted the cities as centres of revolutionary danger, crime and wickedness. The other was hopeful: the condition of the cities gave grounds for assurance that revolution against the injustice of the social and economic order was inevitable. What both these responses neglected, of course, was the accumulating evidence of experience that revolution in Western Europe was in fact less and less likely.

DISORDER AND THE FEAR OF REVOLUTION

The fear of revolution was fed also by disorder, even if its nature was misinterpreted and exaggerated. In Russia, a country which was clearly a part of Europe if it is contrasted with the rest of the world, but one which had not moved forward rapidly along the lines of economic and social progress, reform had not modified autocracy sufficiently and there was a continuing revolutionary movement. It broke out in terrorism – one of whose victims was a tsar – and was supplemented by continuing and spontaneous agrarian unrest. Peasant attacks on landlords and their bailiffs reached a peak in the early years of this

The novel in the 19th century

As a genre, the novel achieved during the 19th century the predominant status it holds today. The great novels of that era constitute an outstanding record of 19th-century society's virtues and vices. Realist writing, in which the circumstances of human life in different social classes were explored, began to become prominent in the 1830s: Honoré de Balzac in France and Charles Dickens in England launched the trend, which later spread throughout the Western world from Leo Tolstoy's Russia to the United States of Henry James. Some of the most significant novels published during the 19th century include:

1813	Jane Austen: *Pride and Prejudice*
1814	Walter Scott: *Waverley*
1825–1827	Alessandro Manzoni: *I Promessi Sposi*
1830	Stendhal: *Le Rouge et le Noir*
1833	Honoré de Balzac: *Eugénie Grandet*
1835	Honoré de Balzac: *Le Père Goriot*
1837	Charles Dickens: *The Pickwick Papers*
1837–1839	Charles Dickens: *Oliver Twist*
1842	Nikolai Gogol: *Dead Souls*
1847	Honoré de Balzac: *La Cousine Bette*
1847	Emily Brontë: *Wuthering Heights*
1851	Herman Melville: *Moby Dick*
1852–1853	Charles Dickens: *Bleak House*
1857	Gustave Flaubert: *Madame Bovary*
1862	Ivan Turgenev: *Fathers and Sons*
1865–1869	Leo Tolstoy: *War and Peace*
1866	Fyodor Dostoyevsky: *Crime and Punishment*
1870	Gustave Flaubert: *L'Education sentimentale*
1871–1872	George Eliot: *Middlemarch*
1875–1877	Leo Tolstoy: *Anna Karenina*
1875	Joao Maria Eça de Queiróz: *Father Amaro's Crime*
1879–1880	Fyodor Dostoyevsky: *The Brothers Karamazov*
1880	Emile Zola: *Nana*
1881	Giovanni Verga: *I Malavoglia*
1884–1885	Leopoldo Alas: *La Regenta*
1885	Emile Zola: *Germinal*
1886	Henry James: *The Bostonians*
1886–1887	Benito Pérez Galdós: *Fortunata y Jacinta*
1895	Thomas Hardy: *Jude the Obscure*
1895	Stephen Crane: *The Red Badge of Courage*
1895	Theodor Fontane: *Effi Briest*
c.1899	Thomas Mann: *Buddenbrooks*

SUNDAY MORNING
WORKMANS HOME
LEATHER LANE

Published in 1875, this image of a London worker's home illustrated a magazine article denouncing the miserable conditions in which many labourers and their families lived.

At the end of the 19th century a wave of anarchist attacks took place across Europe – the aftermath of an explosion at the Véry restaurant in Paris on 25 April, 1892, is seen here. This attack led to the detention of François Ravachol, who was later executed for several terrorist crimes.

century. When they were followed by defeat in war at the hands of the Japanese and the momentary shaking of the régime's confidence, the result was a revolution in 1905. Russia might be, and no doubt was, a special case, but Italy, too, had something that some observers thought of as barely

contained revolution in 1898 and again in 1914, while one of the great cities of Spain, Barcelona, exploded into bloody street-fighting in 1909. Strikes and demonstrations could become violent in industrialized countries without revolutionary traditions, as the United States amply showed in the 1890s; even in Great Britain deaths sometimes resulted from them. This was the sort of data which, when combined with the sporadic activities of anarchists, kept policemen and respectable citizens on their toes. The anarchists especially succeeded in pressing themselves on the public imagination. Their acts of terrorism and assassinations during the 1890s received wide publicity; the importance of such acts transcended success or failure because the growth of the press had meant that great publicity value could be extracted from a bomb or a dagger-stroke. In using such methods, not all anarchists shared the same aims, but they were children of their

ALTROFF

VINS · RESTAURANT · CAFÉ

M. BONAL FILS

epoch: they protested not only against the state in its governmental aspects, but also against a whole society which they judged unjust.

THE SOCIALIST MOVEMENT

SOCIALISTS CONTRIBUTED most to the rhetoric which sustained the fear of revolution. By 1900 socialism almost everywhere meant Marxism. An important alternative tradition and mythology existed only in England, where the early growth of a numerous trade-union movement and the possibility of working through one of the major established political parties produced a non-revolutionary radicalism. The supremacy of Marxism among continental socialists, by contrast, was formally expressed in 1896, when the "Second International", an international working-class movement set up seven years before to coordinate socialist action in all countries, expelled the anarchists who had until then belonged to it. There was a well-established tradition of hostility between anarchism and the Marxism which increasingly dominated socialist organizations. Four years later, the International opened a permanent office in Brussels. Within this movement, numbers, wealth and theoretical contributions made the German Social Democratic Party preponderant. This party had prospered in spite of police persecution thanks to Germany's rapid industrialization, and by 1900 was an established fact of German politics, their first truly mass organization. Its numbers and wealth alone would have made it likely that Marxism, the official creed of the German party, would be that of the international socialist movement, even had Marxism not had its own intellectual and emotional appeal. This appeal lay above all in its assurance that the world was going the way

socialists hoped, and the emotional satisfaction it provided of participating in a struggle of classes, which, Marxists insisted, must end in violent revolution.

REVISIONIST MARXISTS

Though Marxist mythology confirmed the fears of the established order, some intelligent Marxists had noticed that after 1880 or so the facts by no means obviously supported it. Manifestly, great numbers of people had been able to obtain a higher standard of living within the capitalist system. The unfolding of that system in all its complexity was not simplifying and sharpening class conflict in the

In their union building in Milan in 1905, railway workers vote on whether to take strike action. Trade unions had formed in several countries by this time. Many were legally recognized and had their own premises and press.

Jean Jaurès (1859–1914), the founder of the French Socialist Party, is depicted speaking in the Chamber of the National Assembly in Paris. In 1904, Jaurès helped to create the socialist newspaper *L'Humanité*, which he edited until his assassination in 1914.

way Marx had predicted. Moreover, capitalist political institutions had been able to serve the working class. This was very important; in Germany, above all, but also in England, important advantages had been won by socialists using the opportunities provided by parliaments. The vote was available as a weapon and they were not disposed to ignore it while waiting for the revolution. This led some socialists to attempt to restate official Marxism so as to take account of such trends; they were called "revisionists" and, broadly speaking, they advocated a peaceful advance towards the transformation of society by

socialism. If people liked to call that transformation, when it came, a revolution, then only an argument about usage was involved. Inside this theoretical position and the conflict it provoked was a practical issue which came to a head at the end of the century: whether socialists should or should not sit as ministers in capitalist governments.

SPLITS WITHIN SOCIALISM

The debate which divisions in the socialist movement aroused took years to settle. What emerged in the end was explicit condemnation of revisionism by the Second International while national parties, notably the Germans, continued to act on it in practice, doing deals with the existing system as it suited them. Their rhetoric continued to be about revolution. Many socialists even hoped that this might be made a reality by refusing to fight as conscripts if their governments tried to make them go to war. One socialist group, the majority in the Russian party, continued vigorously to denounce revisionism and advocate violence; no doubt this recognized the peculiarity of the Russian situation, where there was little opportunity for effective parliamentary activity and a deep tradition of revolution and terrorism. This group was called Bolshevik, from the Russian word meaning a majority, and more was to be heard of it.

INDUSTRIAL CONSERVATISM AND STATE INTERFERENCE

Socialists claimed to speak for the masses. Whether they did so or did not, by 1900 many conservatives worried that the advances gained by liberalism and democracy in the nineteenth century might well prove irresistible except by force. A few of them were still living in a mental world which was pre-nineteenth rather than pre-twentieth century. In much of Eastern Europe quasi-patriarchal relationships and the traditional authority of the landowner over his estates were still intact. Such societies could still produce aristocratic conservatives who were opposed in spirit not merely to encroachments upon their material privilege, but also to the values and assumptions of what was to be called "market society". But this line was more and more blurred and, for the most part, conservative thinking tended to fall back upon the defence of capital, a position which, of course, would in many places half a century earlier have been regarded as radically liberal, because individualist. The new form of capitalist, industrial conservatism opposed itself more and more vigorously to the state's interference with its wealth, an interference which had grown steadily with

the state's acceptance of a larger and larger role in the regulation of society. There was a crisis in England on the issue which led to a revolutionary transformation of what was left of the 1688 constitution in 1911 by the crippling of the power of the House of Lords to restrain an elected House of Commons. In the background were many issues, among them higher taxation of the rich to pay for social services. Even France had by 1914 accepted the principle of an income tax.

WOMEN IN A CHANGING SOCIETY

CONSTITUTIONAL CHANGES registered the logic of the democratizing of politics in advanced societies. By 1914, universal adult male suffrage existed in France, Germany and several smaller European countries; Great Britain and Italy had electorates big enough

Telephone switchboard operators are shown at work in France at the turn of the century. As more and more jobs became available to women and their traditional role in society began to change, their demand to be enfranchised won support in many European countries.

to come near to meeting this criterion. This brought forward another disruptive question: if men had, should not women have the vote in national politics? The issue was already causing uproar in English politics. But in Europe only Finland and Norway had women in their parliamentary electorates by 1914, though, further afield, New Zealand, two Australian states and some in the United States had given women the franchise by then. The issue was to remain open in many countries for another thirty years.

THE EARLY FEMINIST MOVEMENT

Political rights were only one side of the whole question of women's rights in a society whose overall bias, like that of every other great civilization which had preceded it, was towards the interests and values of men. Yet discussion of women's role in society had begun in the eighteenth century and it was not long before cracks appeared in the structure of assumptions which had so long

Feminism

Women have been subjected to masculine supremacy in virtually every civilization, including those of the Western world. Women's natural role was long perceived to be that of the home-maker; their participation in public affairs was, at best, limited and their freedom of action was restricted by being under the tutelage of their fathers or husbands. Criticism of this inequality began in the atmosphere of intellectual and social change that accompanied the French Revolution. Among the first publications to advocate a new social role for women were *On the Admission of Women to the Right to Sovereignty* (1790) by the Marquis de Condorcet, *Declaration of the Rights of Women and Citizens* (1791) by Olympia de Gouges and *A Vindication of the Rights of Women* (1792) by Mary Wollstonecraft. However, even the Assemblies of revolutionary France did not support greater freedom for women and the Civil Code drawn up under Napoleon perpetuated discrimination.

The situation began to change from the mid-19th century, and particularly during the 20th century. At least in the Western world, women have gradually achieved civil and political equality, access to higher education and to better-paid jobs, and a greater personal freedom, although many believe that this process is not yet complete. The right to vote, which was an essential vindication of the early feminists, was first obtained in some of the world's youngest states: the North American territory of Wyoming (1869), the British dominions of New Zealand (1893) and Australia (1902) and the newly independent Norway (1913).

A feminist protest in France in 1908 is depicted on the cover of a magazine. French women did not obtain the right to vote until after the Second World War.

enclosed it. Women's rights to education, to employment, to control of their own property, to moral independence, even to wear more comfortable clothes, had increasingly been debated in the nineteenth century. Ibsen's play *A Doll's House* was interpreted as a trumpet-call for the liberation of women instead of, as the author intended, a plea for the individual. The bringing forward of such issues implied a real revolution. The claims of women in Europe and North America threatened assumptions and attitudes which had not merely centuries, but even millennia, of institutionalization behind them. They awoke complex emotions, for they were linked to deep-seated notions about the family and sexuality. In these ways, they troubled some people – men and women alike – more deeply than the threat of social revolution or political democracy. People were right to see the question in this dimension. In the early European feminist movement was the seed of something whose explosive content would be even greater when transferred (as it soon was) to other cultures and civilizations assaulted by Western values.

NEW OPPORTUNITIES FOR WOMEN

The politicization of women and political attacks on the legal and institutional structures which were felt by them to be oppressive probably did less for women than did some other changes. Three of these were of slowly growing but, eventually, gigantic importance in undermining tradition. The first was the growth of the advanced capitalist economy. By 1914 this already meant great numbers of new jobs – as typists, secretaries, telephone operators, factory hands, department store assistants and teachers – for women in some countries. Almost none of

these had existed a century earlier. They brought a huge practical shift of economic power to women: if they could earn their own living, they were at the beginning of a road which would eventually transform family structures. Soon, too, the demands of warfare in the industrial societies would accelerate this advance as the need for labour opened an even wider range of occupations to them. Meanwhile, for growing numbers of girls even by 1900, a job in industry or commerce at once meant a chance of liberation from parental regulation and the trap of married drudgery. Most women did not by 1914 so benefit, but an accelerating process was at work, because such developments would stimulate other demands, for example, for education and professional training.

The second great transforming force was even further from showing its full potential to change women's lives by 1914. This was contraception. It had already decisively

This pottery figure of a woman on horseback is entitled *Liberty* and dates from 1905. The figure's dynamism reflects a new vision of women.

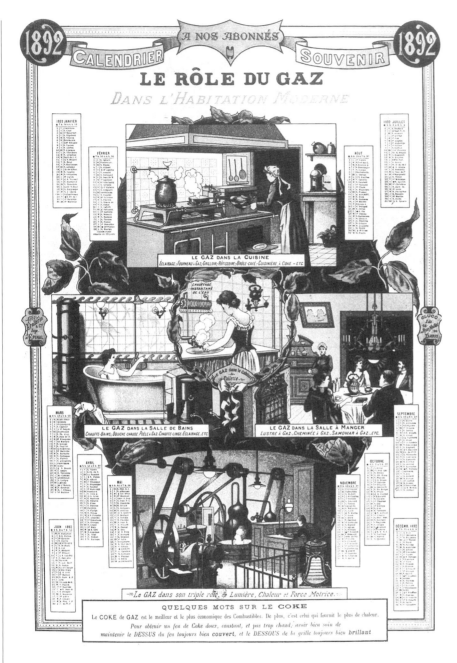

TECHNOLOGY AND WOMEN'S LIBERATION

To the third great tendency moving women imperceptibly but irresistibly towards liberation from ancient ways and assumptions it is much harder to give an identifying single name, but if it has a governing principle, it is technology. It was a process made up of a vast number of innovations, some of them slowly accumulating already for decades before 1900 and all tending to cut into the iron time-tables of domestic routine and drudgery, however marginally at first. The coming of piped water, or of gas for heating and lighting, are among the first examples; electricity's cleanliness and flexibility was later to have even more obvious effects. Better shops were the front line of big changes in retail distribution which not only gave a notion of luxury to people other than the rich, but also made it easier to meet household needs. Imported food, with its better processing and preserving, slowly changed habits of family catering once based – as they are still often based in India or Africa – on daily or twice daily visits to the market. The world of detergents and easily cleaned artificial fibres still lay in the future in 1900, but already soap and washing soda were far more easily and cheaply available than a century before, while the first domestic machines – gas cookers, vacuum cleaners, washing machines – began to make their appearance at least in the homes of the rich early in this century.

FEMALE SUFFRAGE

Historians who would recognize at once the importance of the introduction of the stirrup or the lathe in earlier times have none the less strangely neglected the cumulative force of such humble commodities and instruments as

An advertising poster from 1892 shows the various ways in which gas could be used in the modern home. The consumption of gas was on the increase: it was used to power machines, to provide light and heat in houses and to cook food.

affected demography. What lay ahead was a revolution in power and status as more women absorbed the idea that they might control the demands of childbearing and rearing which hitherto had throughout history dominated most women's lives; beyond that lay an even deeper change, only beginning to be discerned in 1914, as women came to see that they could pursue sexual satisfaction without necessarily entering the obligation of lifelong marriage.

A suffragette is arrested by police after chaining herself to the railings of London's Buckingham Palace in 1914. The campaign for women's suffrage provoked unexpectedly powerful reactions in Britain on both sides of the debate. Women over the age of 30 in the United Kingdom were finally granted the vote in 1918.

these. Yet they implied a revolution for half the world. It is more understandable that their long-term implications interested fewer people at the beginning of this century than the antics of the "suffragettes", as women who sought the vote were called in England.

The immediate stimulus to their activity was the evident liberalization and democratization of political institutions in the case of men. This was the background which their campaign presupposed. Logically, there were grounds for pursuing democracy across the

This contemporary magazine illustration shows campaigners putting up election propaganda posters in Milan in 1911. Political propaganda techniques were inspired by the wider access to the vote and greater literacy.

boundaries of sex even if this meant doubling the size of electorates.

NEW MASS POLITICS

The formal and legal structure of politics was not the whole story of their tendency to show more and more of a "mass" quality. The masses had to be organized. By 1900 there had appeared to meet this need the modern political party, with its simplifications of issues in order to present them as clear choices, its apparatus for the spread of political awareness, and its cultivation of special interests. From Europe and the United States it spread round the world. Old-fashioned politicians deplored the new model of party

and by no means always did so insincerely, because it was another sign of the coming of mass society, the corruption of public debate and the need for traditional élites to adapt their politics to the ways of the man in the street.

The importance of public opinion had begun to be noticed in England early in the nineteenth century. It had been thought decisive in the struggles over the Corn Laws. By 1870, the French emperor felt he could not resist the popular clamour for a war which he feared and was to lose. Bismarck, the quintessential conservative statesman, felt he must give way to public opinion and promote Germany's colonial interests. The manipulation of public opinion, too, seemed to have become possible (or so, at least, many newspaper owners and statesmen believed). Growing literacy had two sides to it. It had been believed on the one hand that investment in mass education was necessary in order to civilize the masses for the proper use of the vote. What seemed to be the consequence of rising literacy, however, was that a market was created for a new cheap press which often pandered to emotionalism and sensationalism, and for the sellers and devisers of advertising campaigns, another invention of the nineteenth century.

NATIONALISM

THE POLITICAL PRINCIPLE which undoubtedly still had the most mass appeal was nationalism. Moreover, it kept its revolutionary potential. This was clear in a number of places. In Turkish Europe, from the Crimean War onwards, the successes of nationalists in fighting Ottoman rule and creating new nations had never flagged. Serbia, Greece and Romania were solidly established by 1870. By the end of the century they had been joined by Bulgaria and Montenegro. In 1913, in the last wars of the Balkan states against Turkey before a European conflict swallowed the Turkish question, there appeared Albania, and by then an autonomous Crete already had a Greek governor. These nationalist movements had at several times dragged greater states into their affairs and always presented a potential danger to peace. This was not so true of those within the Russian Empire, where Poles, Jews, Ukrainians and Lithuanians felt themselves oppressed by the Russians. War, though, seemed a more likely outcome of strains in the Austro-Hungarian Empire, where nationalism presented a real revolutionary danger in the lands within the Hungarian half of the monarchy. Slav majorities there looked across the border to Serbia for help against Magyar oppressors. Elsewhere in the empire – in Bohemia and Slovakia, for example – feeling was less high, but nationalism was no less the dominant question. Great Britain faced no such dangers as these, but even she had a nationalist problem, in Ireland. Indeed, she had two.

Ottoman decline and the emergence of modern Turkey 1683–1923

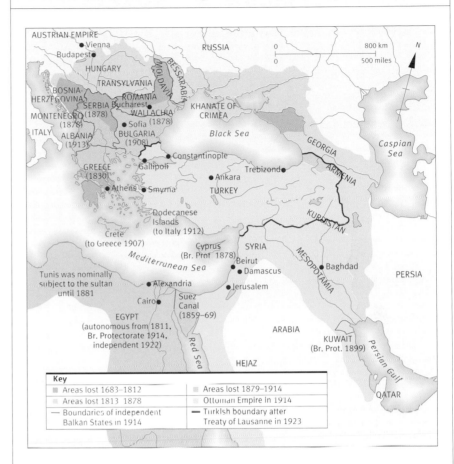

Key

■ Areas lost 1683–1812		■ Areas lost 1879–1914	
■ Areas lost 1813–1878		■ Ottoman Empire in 1914	
— Boundaries of independent Balkan States in 1914		— Turkish boundary after Treaty of Lausanne in 1923	

From the late 17th century, the extent of the Ottoman Empire had been reduced, first at the hands of Austria in the Danube valley, and then around the Black Sea by Russia. The Serbian uprising of 1815–1817 led to the Ottoman retreat from the Balkans, which ended in defeat in the wars of 1912–1913. The North African Ottoman territories were seized by the European countries and, at the end of the First World War, the empire lost the remainder of its Arabian lands.

On the above map some of the areas shown as lost include tributary peoples over whom the Ottomans claimed suzerainty, as well as areas of direct Ottoman rule.

That of the Catholic Irish was for most of the nineteenth century the more obvious. Important reforms and concessions had been granted, though they fell short of the autonomous state of "Home Rule" to which

A massacre of Armenians in Turkey is depicted in an Italian illustration dated 1909. The Young Turks' revolt of 1908 was a major step in the modernization of Turkey, but the nationalist fervour which accompanied it had tragic consequences for the Armenian population.

the British Liberal Party was committed. By 1900, however, agricultural reform and better economic conditions had drawn much of the venom from this Irish question. It was reinserted by the appearance of another Irish nationalism, that of the Protestant majority of the province of Ulster, which was excited to threaten revolution if the government in London gave Home Rule to the Roman Catholic Irish nationalists. This was much more than merely embarrassing. When the machinery of English democracy did finally deliver Home Rule legislation in 1914, some foreign observers were misled into thinking that British policy would be fatally inhibited from intervention in European affairs by revolution at home.

THE GERMAN THREAT

All those who supported expressions of nationalism believed themselves with greater

Kaiser Wilhelm II in 1900. Emperor of Germany from 1888 until 1918, Wilhelm favoured an aggressive foreign policy which contributed to the outbreak of the First World War.

or less justification to do so on behalf of the oppressed. But the nationalism of the great powers was also a disruptive force. France and Germany were psychologically deeply sundered by the transfer of two provinces, Alsace and Lorraine, to Germany in 1871. French politicians whom it suited to do so, long and assiduously cultivated the theme of *revanche*. Nationalism in France gave especial bitterness to political quarrels because they seemed to raise questions of loyalty to great national institutions. Even the supposedly sober British from time to time grew excited about national symbols. There was a brief but deep enthusiasm for imperialism and always great sensitivity over the preservation of British naval supremacy. More and more this appeared to be threatened by Germany, a power whose obvious economic dynamism caused alarm by the danger it presented to British supremacy in world commerce. It did not matter that the two countries were one another's best customers; what was more important was that they appeared to have interests opposed in many specific ways. Additional colour was given to this by the stridency of German nationalism under the reign of the emperor, Wilhelm II. Conscious of Germany's potential, he sought to give it not only real but symbolic expression. One effect was his enthusiasm for building a great navy; this especially annoyed the British who could not see that it could be intended for use against anyone but them. But there was a generally growing impression in Europe, far from unjustified, that the Germans were prone to throw their weight about unreasonably in international affairs. National stereotypes cannot be summarized in a phrase, but because they helped to impose terrible simplifications upon public reactions they are part of the story of the disruptive power of nationalist feeling at the beginning of the twentieth century.

The pre-war belief that any conflict would be limited by its cost turned out to be unfounded. European industry supplied the armies with an unprecedented number of weapons; this image of a British armaments factory during the First World War gives some idea of the immense output. At the same time, the mass conscription of men led to the incorporation of women into manufacturing sectors where they had not previously been employed.

"CIVILIZED WARFARE"

Those who felt confident could point to the diminution of international violence in the nineteenth century; there had been no war between European great powers since 1876 (when Russia and Turkey had come to blows) and, unhappily, European soldiers and statesmen failed to understand the portents of the American Civil War, the first in which one commander could control over a million men, thanks to railway and telegraph, and the first to show the power of modern mass-produced weapons to inflict huge casualties. While such facts were overlooked, the summoning of congresses in 1899 and 1907 to halt competition in armaments could be viewed optimistically, though they failed in their aim. Certainly acceptance of the practice of international arbitration had grown and some restrictions on the earlier brutality of warfare were visible. A significant phrase was used by the German emperor when he sent off his contingent to the international force fielded against the Chinese Boxers. Stirred to anger by reports of atrocities against Europeans by Chinese, he urged his soldiers to behave "like Huns". The phrase stuck in people's memories. Though thought to be excessive even at the time, its real interest lies in the fact that he should have believed such a recommendation was needed. Nobody would have had to tell a seventeenth-century army to behave like Huns, because it was in large measure then taken for granted that they would. By 1900, European troops were not expected to behave in this way and had therefore to be told to do so. So far had the humanizing of war come.

"Civilized warfare" was a nineteenth-century concept and far from a contradiction in terms. In 1899 it had been agreed to forbid, albeit for a limited period, the use of poison gas, dum-dum bullets and even the dropping of bombs from the air.

THE CHURCH IN DECLINE

THE RESTRAINT EXERCISED on European rulers by the consciousness of any unity other than that of a common resistance to revolution had, of course, long since collapsed together with the idea of Christendom. Nineteenth-century religion was only a palliative or mitigation of international conflict, a minor and indirect force, trickling through to a humanitarianism and pacifism fed from other sources. Christianity had proved as feeble a check to violence as would the hopes of socialists that the workers of the world would refuse to fight one another in the interests of their masters. Whether this was a result of a general loss of power by organized religion is not clear. Certainly much misgiving was felt by 1900 about its declining force as an agent regulating behaviour. This was not because a new religion of traditional form challenged the old Christian Churches. There had been, rather, a continuing development of trends observable in the eighteenth century and much more marked since the French Revolution. Almost all the Christian communions seemed more and more touched by the blight of one or other of the characteristic intellectual and social advances of the age. Nor did they seem able to exploit new devices – the late nineteenth-century appearance of mass-circulation newspapers, for instance – which might have helped them. Indeed, some of them, above all the Roman Catholic Church, positively distrusted such developments.

Pius IX was Pope from 1846 to 1878, at a time when the Church of Rome seemed to repudiate the new liberal civilization. He condemned liberalism in the Syllabus of 1864 and refused to accept the incorporation of the Papal States into the newly united Italy.

THE PAPACY LOSES PRESTIGE

Though all the Christian communions felt a hostile current, the Roman Catholic Church was the most obvious victim, the papacy having especially suffered both in its prestige and power. It had openly proclaimed its hostility to progress, rationality and liberalism in statements which became part of the dogmas of the Church. Politically, Rome had begun to suffer from the whittling away of the Temporal Power in the 1790s, when the French revolutionary armies brought revolutionary principles and territorial change to Italy. Often, later infringements of the papacy's rights were to be justified in terms of the master-ideas of the age: democracy, liberalism, nationalism. Finally, in 1870, the last territory of the old Papal States still outside the Vatican itself was taken by the new kingdom of Italy and the papacy became almost entirely a purely spiritual and ecclesiastical authority. This was the end of an era of temporal authority stretching back to Merovingian times and some felt it to be an inglorious one for an institution long the centre of European civilization and history.

In fact, it was in some ways to prove advantageous. Nevertheless, at the time the spoliation confirmed both the hostility to the forces of the century which the papacy had already expressed and the derision in which it was held by many progressive thinkers. Feeling on both sides reached new heights when in 1870 it became a part of the dogma of the Church that the pope, when he spoke *ex cathedra* on faith and morals, did so with infallible authority. There followed two decades in which anticlericalism and priest-baiting were more important in the politics of Germany, France, Italy and Spain than ever before. Governments took advantage of anti-papal prejudice to advance their own legal powers over the Church, but they were also increasingly pushing into areas where the Church had previously been paramount – above all, elementary and secondary education.

Persecution bred intransigence. In conflict, it emerged that whatever view might be taken on the abstract status of the teachings of the Roman Church, it could still draw on vast reservoirs of loyalty among the faithful. Moreover, these were still being recruited by conversion in the mission field overseas and would soon be added to in still greater numbers by demographic trends. Though the Church might not make much progress among the new city-dwellers of Europe, untouched by an inadequate ecclesiastical machine and paganized by the slow stain of the secular culture in which they were immersed, it was far from dying, let alone

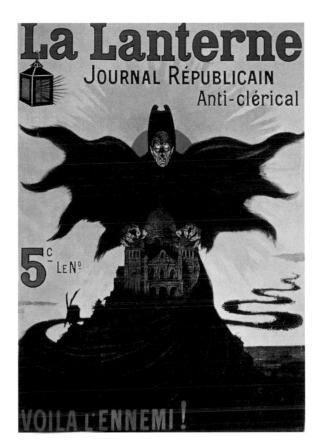

La Lanterne
JOURNAL RÉPUBLICAIN
Anti-clérical

5^c LE N°

VOILA L'ENNEMI!

This anticlerical French cartoon illustrates the confrontation between the Church and its opponents that played a key role in political and intellectual life in the 19th and early 20th centuries.

dead, as a political and social force. Indeed, the liberation of the papacy from its temporal role made it easier for Catholics to feel uncompromised loyalty towards it.

THE QUESTIONING OF TRADITIONAL BELIEFS

The Roman Catholic Church had been the most demanding of the Christian denominations and was in the forefront of the battle of religion with the age, but the claims of revelation and the authority of priest and clergyman were everywhere questioned. This was one of the most striking features of the nineteenth century, all the more so because so many Europeans and Americans still retained simple and literal beliefs in the dogmas of their churches and the story contained in the Bible. They felt great anxiety when such beliefs were threatened, yet this was happening increasingly and in all countries. Traditional religious belief was at first threatened only among an intellectual élite, often consciously holding ideas drawn from Enlightenment sources: "Voltairean" was a favourite nineteenth-century adjective to indicate anti-religious and sceptical views. As the nineteenth century proceeded, such ideas were reinforced by two other intellectual currents, both also at first a concern of élites, but increasingly with a wider effect in an age of growing mass literacy and cheap printing.

What is a nation?

The liberal concept of a nation – seen as a community based not on race or language but on the popular will of people prepared to work together towards a common goal – was expounded in a speech by Ernest Renan:

"A nation is a great solidarity, created by the sense of sacrifices which have been made and those which people are prepared to make in the future. It presupposes a past; but it is summarized in the present in a concrete fact: the consent, the desire freely expressed, to continue to live together. A nation's existence is a daily plebiscite, the same as the existence of an individual is a perpetual affirmation of life … . It will be objected that secession and eventually the decline of nations would be the consequences of a system which leaves old organizations at the mercy of the will of people who are often unenlightened. Clearly, in matters such as this, no principle can be taken to extremes … nations are not eternal. They had a beginning and they will probably have an end. They will probably be replaced by a European confederation. But this is not the law of the century in which we live. At present, the existence of nations is good and even necessary."

An extract from *What is a Nation?* by Ernest Renan, 1882.

The first of these influential groups of ideas came from biblical scholars, the most important of them German, who from the 1840s onwards not only demolished many assumptions about the value of the Bible as historical evidence, but also, and perhaps more fundamentally, brought about something of a psychological change in the whole attitude to the scriptural text. In essence this change made it possible henceforth simply to regard the Bible as a historic text like any other, to be approached critically. An immensely successful (and scandal-provoking) *Life of Jesus*, published in 1863 by a French scholar, Ernest Renan, brought such an attitude before a wider public than ever before. The book which had been the central text of European civilization since its emergence in the Dark Ages would never recover its position.

THE ROLE OF SCIENCE

THE SECOND SOURCE of ideas damaging to traditional Christian faith – and therefore to the morality, politics, and economics for so long anchored in Christian assumptions – was to be found in science. Enlightenment attacks on internal and logical inconsistency in the teaching of the Church became much more alarming when science began to produce empirical evidence that things said in the Bible (and therefore based on the same authority as everything else in it) plainly did not fit observable fact. The starting-point was geology; ideas which had been about since the end of the eighteenth century were given a much wider public in the 1830s by the publication of *Principles of Geology* by Scotch scientist Charles Lyell. This book explained landscape and geological structure in terms of forces still at work, that is, not as the result of a single act of creation,

Darwin's theory of evolution

"It is interesting to contemplate a tangled bank, clothed with many plants of many kinds, with birds singing on the bushes, with various insects flitting about, and with worms crawling through the damp earth, and to reflect that these elaborately constructed forms, so different from each other, and dependent upon each other in so complex a manner, have all been produced from laws acting around us. These laws, taken in the largest sense, being Growth and Reproduction; Inheritance which is almost implied by reproduction; Variability from the indirect and direct action of the conditions of life, and from use and disuse: a ratio of increase so high as to lead to a struggle for life, and as a consequence to Natural Selection, entailing divergence of character and the extinction of less improved forms. Thus, from the war of nature, from famine and death, the most exalted object which we are capable of conceiving, namely, the production of the higher animals, directly follows. There is grandeur in this view of life, with its several powers, having been originally breathed by the Creator into a few forms or into one; and that, whilst this planet has gone cycling on according to the fixed law of gravity, from so simple a beginning endless forms most beautiful and most wonderful have been, and are being evolved."

An extract from the concluding chapter of *The Origin of Species* by Charles Darwin, 1876.

bones of extinct animals. The argument that the human race was much older than the biblical account allowed may perhaps be regarded as officially conceded when, in 1859, British learned societies heard and published papers establishing "that in a period of antiquity remote beyond any of which we have hitherto found traces" human beings had lived in Palaeolithic societies in the Somme valley.

CHARLES DARWIN

It is an over-simplification, but not grossly distorting, to say that the year 1859 brought many of these questions to a head by an approach along a different line, the biological, when an English scientist, Charles Darwin, published one of the seminal books

Charles Darwin (1809–1882) revolutionized concepts about living beings. He applied his theory of evolution, which had first been published in 1859, specifically to the human species in 1871.

but of wind, rain and so on. Moreover, Lyell pointed out that if this were correct, then the presence of fossils of different forms of life in different geological strata implied that the creation of new animals had been repeated in each geological age. If this were so, the biblical account of creation was clearly in difficulties. That biblical chronology was simply untrue in relation to humanity was increasingly suggested by discoveries of stone tools in British caves along with the fossilized of modern civilization, the book called, for short, *The Origin of Species*. Much in it he owed without acknowledgment to others. Its publication came at a moment and in a country where it was especially likely to cause a stir; the issue of the rightfulness of the traditional dominance of religion (for example, in education) was in the air. The word "evolution" with which Darwin's name came especially to be connected was by then already familiar, though he tried to avoid using it and did not let it appear in *The Origin of Species* until its fifth edition, ten years after the first. Nevertheless, his book was the greatest single statement of the evolutionary hypothesis – namely, that living things were what they were because their forms had undergone long evolution from simpler ones. This, of course, included human beings, as he made explicit in another book, *The Descent of Man*, of 1871. Different views were held about how this evolution had occurred. Darwin, impressed by Malthus' vision of the murderous competition of humanity for food, took the view that the qualities which made success likely in hostile environments ensured the "natural selection" of those creatures embodying them: this was a view to be vulgarized (and terribly misrepresented) by the use as a slogan of the phrase "survival of the fittest". But important though many aspects of his work were to be in inspiring fresh thought, here it is important rather to see that Darwin dealt a blow against the biblical account of creation (as well as against the assumption of the unique status of the human race) which had wider publicity than any earlier one. In combination with biblical criticism and geology, his book made it impossible for any conscientious and thoughtful reader to accept – as he or she had still been able to do in 1800 – the Bible as literally true.

THE NEW STATUS OF SCIENCE

The undermining of the authority of scripture remains the most obvious single way in which science affected formulated beliefs. Yet just as important, if not more so, was a new, vague but growing prestige which science was coming to have among a public more broadly-based than ever before. This was because of its new status as the supreme instrument for the manipulation of nature, which was seen as increasingly powerless to resist. Here was the beginning of what was to grow into a mythology of science. Its essence lay in the fact that while the great achievements of seventeenth-century science had not often resulted in changes in the lives of ordinary men and women, those of the nineteenth century increasingly did. People who understood not a word of what might be written by Joseph Lister, who established the need for (and technique of using) antiseptics in surgery, or by Michael Faraday, who more than anyone else made possible the generation of electricity, knew none the less that the medicine of 1900 was different from that of their grandparents and often saw electricity about them in their work and homes. By

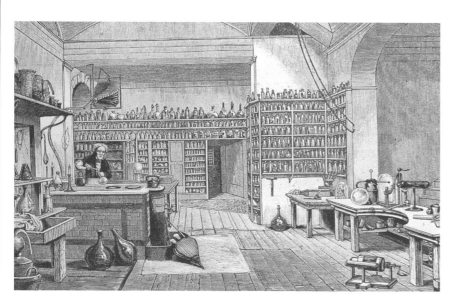

The British physicist Michael Faraday (1791–1867), depicted here in his laboratory, advanced the study of electricity and its possible practical applications considerably when he discovered the law of electromagnetic induction in 1831.

1914, radio messages could be sent across the Atlantic, flying-machines which did not rely upon support by bags of gas of lower density than air were common, aspirins were easily available and an American manufacturer was selling the first cheap mass-produced automobile. The objective achievements of science were by no means adequately represented by such facts, but material advance of this sort impressed the average person and led him or her to worship at a new shrine.

Popular awareness of science came through technology because for a long time this was almost the only way in which science had a positive impact on the lives of most people. Respect for it therefore usually grew in proportion to spectacular results in engineering or manufacture and even now, though science makes its impact in other ways, it still makes it very obviously through industrial processes. But though deeply entwined in this way with the dominant world civilization and so interwoven with society, the growth of science meant much more than just a growth of sheer power. In the years down to 1914 the foundations were laid for what would be evident in the second half of the twentieth century, a science which was as much as anything the mainspring of the dominant world culture. So rapid has been the advance to this state of affairs that science has already affected every part of human life while people are still trying to grapple with some of its most elementary philosophical implications.

SCIENTIFIC INSTITUTIONS

The easiest observations of the changing role of science which can be made (and the easiest to take as a starting-point) are those which display its status as a social and material phenomenon in its own right. From the moment

Some major scientific and technological advances 1815–1905	
1815	Theory of light waves, Augustin-Jean Fresnell
1818	Atomic weights, Jöns Berzelius
1827	Law of electrical conductivity, Georg Ohm
1831	Law of electromagnetic induction, Michael Faraday
1835	Telegraph, Samuel Morse
1839	Photography, Louis-Jacques Daguerre
1846	Anaesthetics, William Morton
1847	Rotary printing press, Richard Hoe
1856	First synthetic dye, Sir William Perkin
1859	Theory of evolution, Charles Darwin
1860–1865	Electromagnetics, James Clerk Maxwell
1865	Principles of heredity, Gregor Mendel
1865	Antisepsis, Joseph Lister
1866	Dynamo, Werner von Siemens
1869	Periodic table of the elements, Dimitri Mendeleyev
1870s	Statistical mechanics and thermodynamics, Ludwig Boltzmann
1876	Telephone, Alexander Graham Bell
1878	Incandescent electric lamp, Thomas Edison
1882	Tuberculosis bacillus, Robert Koch
1885	Anti-rabies vaccine, Louis Pasteur
1885	Automobile, Gottlieb Daimler and Carl Benz
1885–1889	Electrical waves, Heinrich Hertz
1895	Cinematograph, Auguste and Louis Lumière
1896	Radio-telegraphy, Guglielmo Marconi
1897	Electron, Sir Joseph Thompson
1898	Isolation of radium, Marie and Pierre Curie
1900	Quantum theory, Max Planck
1901	Mutation theory, Hugo de Vries
1902	Radioactivity, Ernest Rutherford
1903	Aeroplane, Wilbur and Orville Wright
1905	Special theory of relativity, Albert Einstein

when the first great advances in physics were made, in the seventeenth century, science was already a social fact. Institutions were then created in which men came together to study nature in a way which a later age could recognize as scientific, and scientists even then were sometimes employed by rulers to bring to bear their expertise on specific problems. It was noticeable, too, that in the useful arts – and they were more usually called arts than sciences – such as navigation or agriculture, experiment by those who were not themselves practising technicians could make valuable contributions. But a terminological point helps to set this age in perspective and establish its remoteness from the nineteenth century and after: at this time scientists were still called "natural philosophers". The word "scientist" was not invented until about a third of the way through the nineteenth century, when it was felt that there was need to distinguish a rigorous experimental and observational investigation of nature from speculation on it by unchecked reason. Even then, though, there was little distinction for most people between the man who carried out such an investigation and the applied scientist or technologist who was the much more conspicuous representative of science in an age of engineering, mining and manufacturing on an unprecedented scale.

The nineteenth century was none the less the first in which science was taken for granted by the educated as a specialized field of study, whose investigators had professional standing. Its new status was marked by the much larger place given to science in education, both by the creation of new departments at existing universities, and by the setting up in some countries, notably France and Germany, of special scientific and technical institutions. Professional studies, too, incorporated larger scientific components. Such developments accelerated as the effects of science on social and economic life became increasingly obvious. The sum effect was to carry much further an already long-established trend. Since about 1700 there has been a steady and exponential increase in the world population of scientists: their numbers have doubled roughly every fifteen years (which explains the striking fact that ever since then there have always been, at any moment, more scientists alive than dead). For the nineteenth century, other measurements of the growth of science can be used (the establishment of astronomical observatories, for example) and these, too, provide exponential curves.

THE PRACTICAL APPLICATION OF SCIENTIFIC DISCOVERIES

The ever increasing number of scientists underlay the growing control of his environment and the improvement of his life which

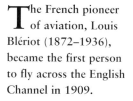

The French pioneer of aviation, Louis Blériot (1872–1936), became the first person to fly across the English Channel in 1909.

were so easily grasped by the layman. This was what made the nineteenth century the first in which science truly became an object of religion – perhaps of idolatry. By 1914, educated Europeans and Americans took for granted anaesthetics, the motor car, the steam turbine, harder and specialized steels, the aeroplane, the telephone, the wireless and many more marvels which had not existed a century previously; their effects were already very great. Perhaps the most widely apparent were those stemming from the availability of cheap electrical power; it was already shaping cities by making electric trams and trains available to suburban householders, work in factories through electric motors, and domestic life through the electric light. Even animal populations were affected: the 36,000 horses pulling trams in Great Britain in 1900 had only 900 successors in 1914. Of course, the practical application of science was by no means new. There has never been a time since the seventeenth century when there has not been some obvious technological fall-out from scientific activity though, to begin with, it was largely confined to ballistics, navigation and map-making, agriculture and a few elementary industrial processes. Only in the nineteenth century did science really begin to play an important role in sustaining and changing society which went beyond a few obviously striking and spectacular accomplishments. The chemistry of dyeing, for example, was a vast field in which nineteenth-century research led to sweeping innovations which flooded through the manufacture of drugs, explosives, antiseptics – to mention only a few. These had human and social, as well as economic, repercussions. The new fast dyes themselves affected millions of people; the unhappy Indian grower of indigo found that his market dried up on him, and the industrial working classes of the West found they could buy marginally less drab clothes and thus began to move slowly forward along the road at the end of which mass-production methods and man-made fibres all but obliterated visible difference between the clothes of different classes.

MEDICAL ADVANCES

This already takes us across the boundary between sustaining life and changing it. Fundamental science was to go on changing society, though some of what was done before 1914 – in physics, for example – is better left for discussion at a later point. One area in which effects are easier to measure was medicine. By 1914, advances had been made which were huge by comparison with a century earlier. A skill had become a science. Great bridgeheads had been driven into the theory and control of infection; antiseptics, having been introduced by Lister only in the

Louis Pasteur (1822–1895) is portrayed carrying out an immunological experiment on a dog. Pasteur discovered anaerobic bacteria and made important contributions to the fight against various infectious diseases, including rabies, for which he produced a vaccine in 1885.

1860s, were taken for granted a couple of decades later, and he and his friend Louis Pasteur, the most famous and greatest of French chemists, laid the foundations of bacteriology. Queen Victoria herself had been a pioneer in the publicizing of new medical methods; the use of anaesthetics during the birth of a prince or princess was important in winning quick social acceptance for techniques only in their infancy in the 1840s. Fewer people, perhaps, would have been aware of the importance of such achievements as the discovery in 1909 of Salvarsan, a landmark in the development of selective treatment of infection, or the identification of the carrier of malaria, or the discovery of "X-rays". Yet all these advances, though of great importance, were to be far surpassed in the next fifty years.

THE MYTHOLOGY OF SCIENCE

Enough impact was made by science even before 1914 to justify the conclusion that it generated its own mythology. In this context, "mythology" implies no connotations of fiction or falsity. It is simply a convenient way of calling attention to the fact that science, the vast bulk of its conclusions no doubt validated by experiment and therefore "true", has also come to act as an influence shaping the way we look at the world, just as great religions have done in the past. It has, that is to say, come to be important as more than a method for exploring and manipulating nature. It has been thought also to provide guidance about metaphysical questions, the aims human beings ought to pursue, the standards they should employ to regulate

These motor cars and omnibuses were photographed in London's Oxford Street in 1911. By that time, although horse-drawn carriages were still the main means of transport in almost every city in the world, the mass production of cheap cars had already begun in the United States.

Science and the idea of progress

The 19th century saw a dramatic improvement in the ability of science to explain the physical and biological world, and to apply the knowledge acquired to the development of technology. This led, in the whole of the Western world and later also in Japan, India and China, to a widespread confidence that many human problems could be solved through scientific reasoning and experimentation.

Thinkers such as Jeremy Bentham (1748–1832), Auguste Comte (1798–1857), Karl Marx (1818–1883) and Herbert Spencer (1820–1903) defended the need to make a scientific study of human behaviour and of society itself. Bentham tried to define the principles of social organization based on measuring human behaviour with respect to pleasure and pain. Marx built a system around deterministic materialism. Comte set down the foundations of positivism and defined sociology as a science. Spencer tried to justify capitalism scientifically by asserting that competition played the same role in human progress as natural selection did in the evolution of the species.

Some dissidents spoke out against such ideas. A leading Darwinist, Thomas Huxley (1825–1895) none the less took the view that human society should be based on totally different rules from those of a brutal natural selection.

behaviour. Above all it has been a pervasive influence in shaping popular attitudes. All this, of course, has no intrinsic or necessary connexion with science as the pursuit of scientists. But the upshot in the end was a civilization whose élites had, except vestigially, no dominant religious belief or transcendent ideals. It is a civilization whose core, whether or not this is often articulated, lies in belief in the promise of what can be done by manipulating nature. In principle, it believes that there is no problem which need be regarded as insoluble, given sufficient resources of intellect and money; it has room for the obscure, but not for the essentially mysterious. Many scientists have drawn back from this conclusion. The implications of it are still far from being grasped. But it is the assumption on which a dominant world view now rests and it was already formed in essentials before 1914.

THE BIRTH OF SOCIOLOGY

Confidence in science in its crudest form has been called "scientism", but probably very few people held it with complete explicitness and lack of qualification, even in the late nineteenth century, its heyday. Equally good evidence of the prestige of the scientific method, though, is provided by the wish shown by intellectuals to extend it beyond the area of the natural sciences. One of the earliest examples can be detected in the wish to found "social sciences" which can be seen in the utilitarian followers of the English reformer and intellectual Jeremy Bentham, who hoped to base the management of society upon calculated use of the principles that people responded to pleasure and pain, and that pleasure should be maximized and pain minimized, it being understood that what was to be taken into account were the sensations of the greatest number and their intensity. Later in the nineteenth century, Marx (who was greatly impressed by the work of Darwin) also exemplified the wish to found a science of society. A name for one was provided by the French philosopher Auguste Comte – sociology. These (and many other) attempts to emulate the natural sciences proceeded on a basis of a search for general quasi-mechanical laws; that the natural sciences were at that moment abandoning the search for such laws does not signify here, the search itself still testifying to the scientific model's prestige.

OLD VALUES RECONSIDERED

Paradoxically, science too was contributing by 1914 to an ill-defined sense of strain in European civilization. This showed most obviously in the problems posed to traditional religion, without doubt, but it also operated in a more subtle way; in determinisms such as those many drew from thinking about Darwin, or through a relativism suggested by anthropology or the study of the human mind, science itself sapped the confidence in the values of objectivity and rationality which had been so important to it since the eighteenth century. By 1914 there were signs that liberal, rational, enlightened Europe was under strain just as much as traditional, religious and conservative Europe.

EUROPEAN INTERRELATIONSHIPS

Doubt must not loom too large. The most obvious fact about early twentieth-century Europe is that although many Europeans might be sceptical or fearful about its future, it was almost never suggested that it would not continue to be the centre of the world's affairs, the greatest concentration of political power in the globe and the real maker of the world's destinies. Diplomatically and politically, European statesmen could ignore the rest of the world for all important matters, except in the western hemisphere, where another nation of European origins, the United States, was paramount, and the Far East, where Japan was increasingly important and the Americans had interests which they might require others to respect. It was their relationships with one another, nevertheless, that fascinated most European statesmen in 1900; for most of them there was nothing else so important to worry about at this time.

This political cartoon mocking the German domination of European diplomacy appeared in a 1908 edition of the British publication *Punch*. Entitled *A Rival Attraction*, the cartoon depicts a neglected artiste (a performer on the European concertina) complaining that she will never have her chance to appear on stage, "what with all these Berlin knock-about extra turns!".

5 *THE ERA OF THE FIRST WORLD WAR*

Emperor Franz Josef attends a ball in Vienna at the beginning of the 20th century. During Franz Josef's reign (1848–1916), the Austrian Empire (which became the Austro-Hungarian Empire in 1867) suffered from fierce nationalist pressures.

AGAINST THE ONE CLEAR favourable fact that great wars had been successfully averted by European states ever since 1870, could be set some political evidence that the international situation was none the less growing dangerously unstable by 1900. Some major states had grave internal problems, for example, which might imply external repercussions. For all the huge difference between them, United Germany and United Italy were new states; they had not existed forty years earlier and this made their rulers especially sensitive to internal divisive forces and consequently willing to court chauvinistic feeling. Some of Italy's leaders went in for disastrous colonial ventures, keeping alive suspicion and unfriendliness towards Austria-Hungary (formally Italy's ally, but the ruler of territories still regarded by Italians as "unredeemed") and finally plunged their country into war with Turkey in 1911. Germany had the advantages of huge industrial and economic success to help her, yet after the cautious Bismarck had been sent into retirement her foreign policy was conducted more and more with an eye to winning the impalpable and slippery prizes of respect and prestige – a "place in the sun", as some Germans summed it up. Germany had also to face the consequences of industrialization. The new economic and social forces it spawned were increasingly difficult to reconcile with the conservative character of her constitution which gave so much weight in imperial government to a semi-feudal, agrarian aristocracy.

PROBLEMS IN RUSSIA

Internal tensions were not confined to new states. The two great dynastic empires of

Time chart (1867–1922)				
	1867 Austro-Hungarian Empire founded	1894 Franco-Russian alliance	1917 Russian Revolution	1918 End of the First World War
1850		1900		1950
	1879 Alliance of Germany and Austria-Hungary		1914 Start of the First World War	1922 Triumph of Fascism in Italy

Russia and Austria-Hungary each faced grave internal problems; more than any other states they still fitted the assumption of the Holy Alliance era that governments were the natural opponents of their subjects. Yet both had undergone great change in spite of apparent continuity. The Habsburg monarchy in its new, hyphenated form was itself the creation of a successful nationalism, that of the Magyars. In the early years of the twentieth century there were signs that it was going to be more and more difficult to keep the two halves of the monarchy together without provoking other nations inside it beyond endurance. Moreover, here, too, industrialization (in Bohemia and Austria) was beginning to add new tensions to old. Russia, as has been indicated, actually exploded in political revolution in 1905, and was also changing more deeply. Autocracy and terrorism between them destroyed the liberal promise of the reforms of Alexander II, but they did not prevent the start of faster industrial growth by the end of the century. This was the beginning of an economic revolution to which the great emancipation had been the essential preliminary. Policies designed to exact grain from the peasant provided a commodity for export to pay for the service of foreign loans. With the twentieth century, Russia began to show at last a formidable rate of economic advance. The quantities were still small – in 1910 Russia produced less than a third as much pig-iron as the United Kingdom and only about a quarter as much steel as Germany. But these quantities had been achieved at a very high rate of growth. Probably more important, there were

The picture shows the Russian squadron in the French Mediterranean port of Toulon, in 1893. The following year, both countries' distrust of Germany led to a Franco-Russian alliance.

A peasant gathering takes place in rural Russia in 1910. The seated man at the left of the picture appears to be literate, which was extremely rare among the rural population at that time.

signs that by 1914 Russian agriculture might at last have turned the corner and be capable of producing a grain harvest which would grow faster than population. A determined effort was made by one minister to provide Russia with a class of prosperous independent farmers whose self-interest was linked to raising productivity, by removing the last of the restraints on individualism imposed by the terms of serfdom's abolition. Yet there was still much backwardness to overcome. Even in 1914 fewer than 10 per cent of Russians lived in towns and only about three million out of a total population of more than one hundred and fifty million worked in industry. The debit side still loomed large in foreign estimates of Russia's progress. She might be a potential giant, but was one entangled with grievous handicaps. The autocracy governed badly, reformed unwillingly and opposed all change (though it was to make constitutional concessions in 1905). The general level of culture was low and unpromising; industrialization would demand better education and that would cause new strains. Liberal traditions were weak; terrorist and autocratic traditions were strong. Russia

was still dependent on foreign suppliers for the capital she needed, too.

FRANCE

Most of Russia's capital came from her ally, France. With the United Kingdom and Italy, the Third Republic represented liberal and constitutional principles among Europe's great powers. Socially conservative, France was, in spite of her intellectual vitality, uneasy and conscious of weakness. In part, a superficial instability was a matter of bitter exchanges between politicians; in part it was because of the efforts of some who strove to keep alive the revolutionary tradition and rhetoric. Yet the working-class movement was weak. France moved only slowly towards industrialization and, in fact, the Republic was probably as stable as any other régime in Europe, but slow industrial development indicated another handicap of which the French were very aware, their military inferiority. The year 1870 had shown that the French could not on their own beat the German army. Since then, the disparity of the two countries' positions had grown ever greater. In manpower, France had fallen further still behind and in economic development, too, she had been dwarfed by her neighbour. Just before 1914, France was raising about one-sixth as much coal as Germany, made less than a third as much pig-iron and a quarter as much steel. If there was ever to be a return match for 1870, the French knew they needed allies.

BRITAIN IN 1900

An ally for France was not, in 1900, to be looked for across the Channel. This was mainly because of colonial issues; France (like

Russia) came into irritating conflict with the United Kingdom in a great many places around the globe where British interests lay. For a long time, the United Kingdom found she could remain clear of European entanglements; this was an advantage, but she, too, had troubles at home. The first industrial nation was also one of the most troubled by working-class agitation and, increasingly, by uncertainty about her relative strength. By 1900 some British businessmen were clear that Germany was a major rival; there were plenty of signs that in technology and method German industry was greatly superior to British. The old certainties began to give way; free trade itself was called in question. There were even signs, in the violence of Ulstermen and suffragettes and the embittered struggles over social legislation with a House of Lords determined to safeguard the interests of wealth, that parliamentarianism itself might be threatened. There was no longer a sense of the sustaining consensus of mid-Victorian politics. Yet there was also a huge solidity about British institutions and political habits. Parliamentary monarchy had proved able to carry through vast changes since 1832 and there was little reason for fundamental doubt that it could continue to do so.

THE GROWING POWER OF THE UNITED STATES

Only a perspective which the British of the day found hard to recognize reveals the fundamental change which had come about in the international position of the United Kingdom within the preceding half-century

The end of an era for Britain came when Queen Victoria, who had reigned for almost 64 years, died in 1901. This photograph shows her funeral cortège passing through the streets of Cowes on the Isle of Wight.

Immigrants continued to flood into the United States after the turn of the century. Those pictured here are arriving at the money exchange on New York's Ellis Island.

or so. This is provided by a view from Japan or the United States, the two great extra-European powers. The Japanese portent was the more easily discerned of the two, perhaps, because of the military victory over Russia, yet there were signs for those who could interpret them that the United States would shortly emerge as a power capable of dwarfing Europe and as the most powerful nation in the world. Her nineteenth-century expansion had come to a climax with the establishment of her supremacy on an unquestionable footing of power in her own hemisphere. The war with Spain and the building of the Panama Canal rounded off the process. American domestic, social and economic circumstances were such that the political system proved easily able to handle the problems it faced once the great mid-century crisis was surmounted. Amongst these, some of the gravest resulted from industrialization. The confidence that all would go well if the economically strongest were simply allowed to drive all others to the wall first began to be questioned towards the end of the nineteenth century. But this was after an industrial machine of immense scale had already matured. It would be the bedrock of future American power. By 1914 American production of pig-iron and steel was more than twice that of Great Britain and Germany together; the United States mined almost enough coal to outpace them, too. At the same time the standard of living of her citizens continued to act as a magnet to immigration; in her natural resources and a stream of cheap, highly motivated labour lay two of the sources of America's economic might. The other was foreign capital. She was the greatest of debtor nations.

Though her political constitution was older in 1914 than that of any major

European state except Great Britain or Russia, the arrival of new Americans long helped to give the United States the characteristics and psychology of a new nation. A need to integrate her new citizens often led to the expression of strong nationalist feeling. But because of geography, a tradition of rejecting Europe, and the continuing domination of American government and business by élites formed in the Anglo-Saxon tradition, this did not take violent forms outside the western hemisphere. The United States in 1914 was still a young giant waiting in the wings of history, whose full importance would only become manifest when Europe needed to involve America in its quarrels.

THE TWO WORLD WARS

IN 1914 A WAR BEGAN as a result of Europe's internal quarrels. Though it was not the bloodiest nor the most prolonged war in history, nor strictly, as it was later termed, the "first" world war, it was the most intensely fought struggle and the greatest in geographical extent to have occurred down to that time. Nations in every continent took part. It was also costlier than any earlier war and made unprecedented demands upon resources. Whole societies were mobilized to fight it, in part because it was also the first war in which machines played an overwhelmingly important part; war was for the first time transformed by science. The best name to give it remains the simple one used by those who fought in it: the *Great* War. This is justified by its unprecedented psychological effect.

It was also the first of two wars whose central issue was the control of German power. The damage they did ended Europe's political, economic and military supremacy. Each of these conflicts began in essentially European issues and the war always had a

predominantly European flavour; like the next great struggle detonated by Germany though, it sucked into it other conflicts and jumbled together a whole anthology of issues. But Europe was the heart of the matter and self-inflicted damage in the end deprived her of world hegemony. This did not happen by 1918, when the Great War ended (though irreparable damage had already been done, even by then), but it was obvious in 1945, at the end of a "second world war". That left behind a continent whose pre-1914 structure had vanished. It has led some historians to speak of the whole era from 1914 to 1945 as an entity, as a European "civil war" – not a bad metaphor, provided it is borne in mind that it is a metaphor. Europe had never been free from wars for long and the containment of internal disorder is the fundamental presupposition of a state: Europe had never been united and could not therefore have a true civil war. But it was the source and seat of a civilization which was a unity; Europeans saw themselves as having more in common with other Europeans than with

This painting shows a Mk V tank going into action in the First World War. Tanks, which could not be stopped by barbed wire and machine-gun fire, were developed by the British and were used for the first time on the Western Front in 1916.

black, brown or yellow peoples. Furthermore, it was a system of power which in 1914 was an economic unity and had just experienced its longest period of internal peace. These facts, all of which were to vanish by 1945, make the metaphor of civil war vivid and acceptable; it signifies the self-destructive madness of a civilization.

A DELICATE PEACE

A European balance had kept the peace between great states for over forty years. By 1914 this was dangerously disturbed. Too many people had come to feel that the chances of war might offer them more than a continued peace. This was especially so in the ruling circles of Germany, Austria-Hungary and Russia. By the time that they had come to

This poster urged British women to encourage their husbands and sons to fight in the First World War. The extensive British propaganda campaign appears to have been almost unnecessary until 1916, such was the level of popular support for the cause. It was not uncommon, for example, for young men to lie about their age in order to be accepted as volunteers. Of those who went to war, however, an unprecedented number never returned – the scale of the slaughter on both sides was enormous.

feel this, there existed a complicated set of ties, obligations and interests between states which so involved them with one another that it was unlikely that a conflict could be limited to two, or even to a few of them. Another force making for instability was the existence of small countries enjoying special relations with larger ones; some of them were in a position to take the effective power to make decisions from the hands of those who would have to fight a major war.

EUROPE COURTS DANGER

The delicate European situation in 1914 was made all the more dangerous by the psychological atmosphere in which statesmen by then had to work. It was an age when mass emotions were easily aroused, in particular by nationalist and patriotic stimuli. There was widespread ignorance of the dangers of war, because nobody except a tiny minority foresaw a war which would be different from that of 1870; they remembered the France of that year, and forgot how, in Virginia and Tennessee only a few years earlier, modern war had first shown its face in prolonged slaughter and huge costs (more Americans died in the Civil War than have died in all the other wars in which the United States has taken part, even to the present day). Everyone knew that wars could be destructive and violent, certainly, but also believed that in the twentieth century they would be swiftly over. The very cost of armaments made it inconceivable that civilized states could sustain a prolonged struggle such as that with Napoleonic France; the complex world economy and the taxpayer, it was said, could not survive one. This perhaps diminished misgivings about courting danger. There are even signs, too, that many Europeans were bored by their lives in 1914 and saw in war an

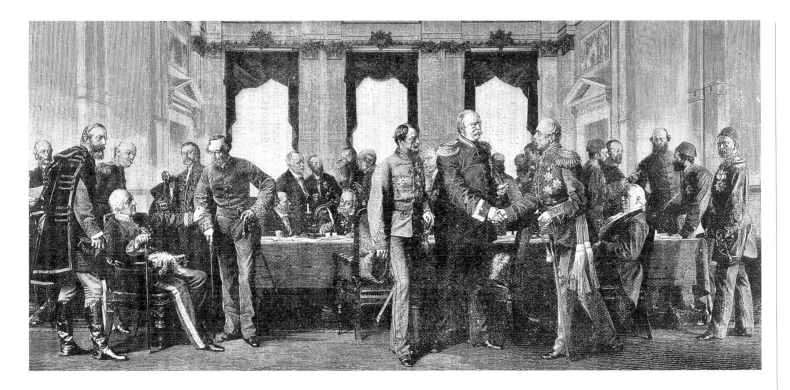

emotional release purging away a sense of decadence and sterility. Revolutionaries, of course, welcomed international conflict because of the opportunities they thought it might bring. Finally, it is worth remembering that the long success of diplomats in negotiating grave crises without war was itself a danger. Their machinery had worked so many times that when it was presented with facts more than ordinarily recalcitrant in July 1914, their significance for a time seemed to escape many of those who had to deal with them. On the very eve of conflict, statesmen were still finding it difficult to see why another conference of ambassadors or even a European congress should not extricate them from their problems.

REVOLUTIONARY NATIONALISM

One of the conflicts which came to a head in 1914 went back a very long way. This was the old rivalry of Austria-Hungary and Russia in southeastern Europe. Its roots lay deep in the eighteenth century, but its last phase was dominated by the accelerated collapse of the Ottoman Empire in Europe from the Crimean War onwards. For this reason the First World War is from one point of view to be seen as another war of the Ottoman succession. After the Congress of Berlin in 1878 had pulled Europe through one dangerous moment, Habsburg and Romanov policy had settled down to a sort of understanding by the 1890s. This lasted until Russian interest in the Danube valley revived after the checking of Russian imperial ambition in the Far East by the Japanese. At that moment, events outside the Habsburg and Turkish empires were giving a new aggressiveness to Austro-Hungarian policy, too.

At the root of this was revolutionary nationalism. A reform movement looked for a while as if it might put the Ottoman empire together again and this provoked the Balkan nations to try to undo the status quo established by the great powers and the Austrians to look to their own interests in a situation once again fluid. They offended the Russians

This contemporary engraving shows the main participants in the 1878 Congress of Berlin. The foreground is dominated by the tall figure of the German chancellor, Prince von Bismarck, who is depicted shaking hands with the Russian representative Count Shuvalov. On the left, shown leaning on his cane, is Benjamin Disraeli, the British prime minister, with Emperor Franz Josef of Austria-Hungary.

by a mismanaged annexation of the Turkish province of Bosnia in 1909; the Russians had not been given a corresponding and compensating gain. Another consequence of Bosnia's annexation was that the Dual Monarchy acquired more Slav subjects. There was already discontent among the monarchy's subject peoples, in particular, the Slavs who lived under Magyar rule. More and more under the pressure of Magyar interests, the government in Vienna had shown itself hostile to Serbia, a nation to which these Slav subjects might look for support. Some of them saw Serbia as the nucleus of a future state embracing all South Slavs, and its rulers seemed unable (and perhaps unwilling) to restrain South Slav revolutionaries who used

This French illustration depicts the assassination in 1903 of the king of Serbia, Alexander I, and his wife. The inset portrays Alexander's successor, Peter I. Internal and external strife made the Balkans the most unstable area in Europe.

Belgrade as a base for terrorism and subversion in Bosnia. Lessons from history are often unfortunate; the Vienna government was only too ready to conclude that Serbia might play in the Danube valley the role that Sardinia had played in uniting Italy. Unless the serpent were scotched in the egg, another loss of Habsburg territory would then follow. Having been excluded from Germany by Prussia and from Italy by Sardinia, a potential Yugoslavia now seemed to some Habsburg counsellors to threaten the empire with exclusion from the lower Danube valley. This would mean its end as a great power and an end, too, of Magyar supremacy in Hungary, for fairer treatment of Slavs who remained in Hungarian territory would be insisted upon by South Slavdom. The continuing subsidence of the Ottoman Empire could then only benefit Russia, the power which stood behind Serbia, determined there should not be another 1909.

EUROPEAN POWERS ARE DRAWN INTO THE CONFLICT

Into this complicated situation, the other powers were pulled by interest, choice, sentiment and formal diplomacy. Of these, the last was perhaps less important than was once thought. Bismarck's efforts in the 1870s and 1880s to ensure the isolation of France and the supremacy of Germany had spawned a system of alliances unique in peacetime. Their common characteristic was that they defined conditions on which countries would go to war to support one another, and this seemed to cramp diplomacy. But in the end they did not operate as planned. This does not mean that they did not contribute to the coming of war, only that formal arrangements can only be effective if people want them to be, and other factors decided that in 1914.

At the root of the whole business was the German seizure of Alsace and Lorraine from France in 1871, and the consequent French restlessness for revenge. Bismarck guarded against this first by drawing together Germany, Russia and Austria-Hungary on the common ground of dynastic resistance to revolutionary and subversive dangers which France, the only republic among the major states, was still supposed to represent; there were still alive in 1871 people born before 1789 and many others who could remember the comments of those who had lived through the years of the great Revolution, while the upheaval of the Paris Commune revived all the old fears of international subversion. The conservative alliance none the less lapsed in the 1880s, essentially because Bismarck felt he must in the last resort back Austria-Hungary if a conflict between her and Russia proved unavoidable. To Germany and the Dual Monarchy was then added Italy; thus was formed in 1882 the Triple Alliance. But Bismarck still kept a separate "Reinsurance" treaty with Russia, though he seems to have felt uneasy about the prospect of keeping Russia and Austria-Hungary at peace in this way.

TWO CAMPS IN EUROPE

A conflict between Russia and Austria-Hungary did not again look likely until after 1909. By then, Bismarck's successors had allowed his Reinsurance treaty to lapse and Russia had become in 1892 an ally of France. From that date the road led away from Bismarck's Europe, where everyone else had been kept in equilibrium by Germany's central role, to a Europe divided into two camps. This was made worse by German policy. In a series of crises, she showed that she wanted to frighten other nations with her

displeasure and make herself esteemed. In particular, in 1905 and 1911 her irritation was directed against France, and commercial and colonial issues were used as excuses to show by displays of force that France had not won the right to disregard German wishes by making an ally of Russia. German military planning had already by 1900 accepted the need to fight a two-front war if necessary, and made preparations to do so by a quick overthrow of France while the resources of Russia were slowly mobilized.

As the twentieth century opened, it had therefore become highly probable that if an Austro-Russian war broke out, Germany and France would join in. Moreover, Germans had within a few years made this more likely by patronizing the Turks. This was much more alarming to the Russians than it would have been earlier, because a growing export trade in grain from Russia's Black Sea ports had to pass through the Straits. The Russians began to improve their fighting-power. One essential step in this was the completion of a railway network which would make possible the mobilization and delivery to the battlefields of Eastern Europe of Russia's vast armies.

Tsar Alexander III of Russia, Emperor Franz Josef of Austria-Hungary and Emperor Wilhelm I of Germany meet at the Warsaw Conference in 1884. Prince von Bismarck, then German chancellor, made great efforts during the conference to maintain the alliance with Russia, which Wilhelm II would later renounce.

BRITISH INVOLVEMENT IN THE CONFLICT

There was no obvious need for Great Britain to be concerned in a potential Austro-Russian struggle, had not German policy perversely antagonized her. At the end of the nineteenth century Great Britain's quarrels were almost all with France and Russia. They arose where imperial ambitions clashed, in Africa and Central and Southeastern Asia. Anglo-German relations were more easily managed, if occasionally prickly. As Great Britain entered the new century she was still preoccupied with empire, not with Europe. The first peacetime alliance she had made since the eighteenth century was with Japan, to safeguard her interests in the Far East. Then came a settlement of long outstanding disputes with France in 1904; this was in essence an agreement about Africa, where France was to be given a free hand in Morocco in return for Great Britain having one in Egypt – a way of settling another bit of the Ottoman succession

– but it rounded up other colonial quarrels the world over, some going back as far as the Peace of Utrecht. A few years later, Great Britain made a similar (though less successful) agreement with Russia about spheres of interest in Persia. But the Anglo-French settlement grew into much more than a clearing away of grounds for dispute. It became what was called an entente, or special relationship.

This was Germany's doing. Irritated by the Anglo-French agreement, the German government decided to show France that it would have to have its say in Morocco's affairs at an international conference. They got it, but bullying France solidified the entente; the British began to realize that they would have to concern themselves for the first time in decades with the continental balance of power. If they did not, Germany would dominate it. At the end of this road would be their acceptance of a role as a great military power on land, a change of the assumptions which British strategy had followed since the days of Louis XIV and Marlborough, the last age in which the country had put its major weight into prolonged effort on the Continent. Secret military talks with the French explored what might be done to help their army against a German invasion through Belgium. This was not going far, but Germany then threw away the chance to reassure British public opinion, by pressing forward with plans to build a great navy. It was inconceivable that such a step could be directed against any power except Great Britain. The result was a naval race which most British were determined to win (if they could not end it) and therefore the further inflammation of popular feeling. In 1911, when the gap between the two countries' fleets was narrowest and most felt in Great Britain, German diplomacy provoked another crisis over Morocco. This time, a British

This cartoon, which appeared in the British publication *Punch* in March 1906 with the caption "Sitting Tight", makes fun of the German attempt to limit French control in Morocco.

Archduke Franz Ferdinand, heir to the Austro-Hungarian crown, is shown with his wife in Sarajevo on 28th June, 1914. Moments after this photograph was taken, both of them were assassinated by a terrorist; the complex reactions to this event led to the outbreak of the First World War.

minister said publicly something that sounded very much like an assertion that Great Britain would go to war to protect France.

THE OUTBREAK OF THE GREAT WAR

When war came, it was in the South Slav lands. Serbia did well in the Balkan Wars of 1912–13, in which the young Balkan nations first despoiled Turkey of most that was left of her European territory and then fell out over the spoils. But Serbia might have got more had the Austrians not objected. Behind Serbia stood Russia, launched on the programme of rebuilding and expanding her forces which would take three or four years to bring to fruition. If South Slavs were to be shown that the Dual Monarchy could humiliate Serbia so that they could not hope for her support, then the sooner the better. Given that Germany was the Dual Monarchy's ally she, in turn, was

unlikely to seek to avoid fighting Russia while there was still time to be sure of winning.

The crisis came when an Austrian archduke was assassinated by a Bosnian terrorist at Sarajevo in June 1914. The Austrians believed that the Serbians were behind it. They decided that the moment had come to teach Serbia her lesson and kill for ever the pan-Slav agitation. The Germans supported them. The Austrians declared war on Serbia on 28 July. A week later all the great powers were at war (though, ironically, the Austro-Hungarians and Russians were still at peace with one another; it was only on 6 August that the Dual Monarchy at last declared war on its old rival). Before that date German military planning had dictated the timetable of events. The key decision to attack France before Russia had been made years before; German planning required such an attack to be made through Belgium, whose neutrality the British among others had guaranteed. Thereafter the sequence of events fell almost

The Great War of 1914–1918

At the start of the First World War, Austria-Hungary and Germany were at war with Serbia, Russia, France, Belgium and Great Britain – other countries joined the conflict as the war progressed. The Western Front was soon established, after an initial German advance, while on the Eastern Front the Austro-Hungarians and Germans managed to occupy Serbia, Romania and some provinces of imperial Russia. Following the Russian Revolution in 1917, after which the Bolsheviks sued for peace in early 1918, the Germans moved most of their troops to the Western Front, where the outcome of the war was eventually decided.

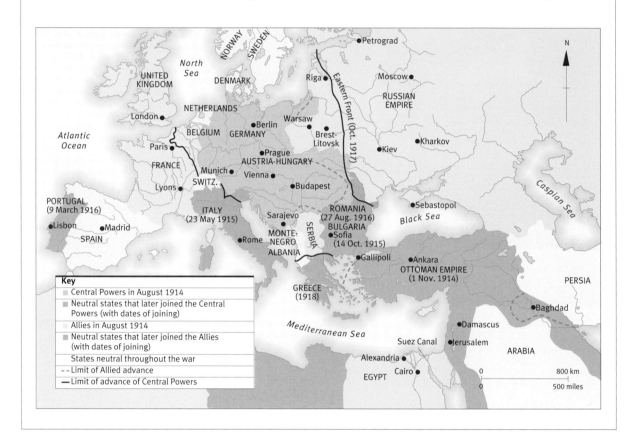

automatically into place. When Russia mobilized to bring pressure on Austria-Hungary for Serbia's protection, the Germans declared war on Russia. Having done that, they had to attack the French and, finding a pretext, formally declared war on them. Thus, the Franco-Russian alliance never actually operated. By Germany's violation of Belgian neutrality, the British government, uneasy about a German attack on France, but not seeing clearly on what grounds they could justify intervention to prevent it, was given an issue to unite the country and take it into war against Germany on 4 August.

THE THEATRE OF WAR

Just as the duration and intensity of the war were to outrun all expectations, so did its geographical spread. Japan and the Ottoman Empire joined in soon after the outbreak; the former on the side of the Allies (as France, Great Britain and Russia were called) and Turkey on that of the Central Powers (Germany and Austria-Hungary). Italy joined the Allies in 1915, in return for promises of Austrian territory. Other efforts were made to pick up new supporters by offering cheques to be cashed after a victorious peace; Bulgaria joined the Central Powers in September 1915 and Romania the Allies in the following year. Greece became another Allied state in 1917. Portugal's government had tried to enter the war in 1914, but though unable to do so because of internal troubles was finally faced with a German declaration of war in 1916. Thus, by the end of that year, the original issues of Franco-German and Austro-Russian rivalry had been thoroughly confused by other struggles. The Balkan states were fighting a third Balkan war (the war of the Ottoman succession in its European theatre), the British a war against German naval and commercial power, the Italians the last war of the Risorgimento, while outside Europe the British, Russians and Arabs had begun a war of Ottoman partition in Asia and the Japanese were pursuing another cheap and highly profitable episode in the assertion of their hegemony in the Far East.

A NEW KIND OF WARFARE

One reason why there was a search for allies in 1915 and 1916 was that the war then showed every sign of bogging down in a stale-mate no one had expected. The nature of the fighting had surprised almost everyone. It had opened with a German sweep into northern France. This did not achieve the lightning victory which was its aim but gave the Germans possession of all but a tiny scrap of Belgium and much French territory, too. In the east, Russian offensives had been stopped by the Germans and Austrians. Thereafter, though more noticeably in the west than the east, the battlefields settled down to siege warfare on an unprecedented scale. This was because of two things. One was the huge killing-power of modern weapons. Magazine rifles, machine-guns and barbed wire could stop any infantry attack not preceded by

pulverizing bombardment. Demonstrations of this truth were provided by the huge casualty lists. By the end of 1915 the French army alone had lost 300,000 dead; that was bad enough, but in 1916 one seven-month battle before Verdun added another 315,000 to this total. In the same battle 280,000 Germans died. While it was going on, another struggle further north, on the Somme, cost the British 420,000 casualties and the Germans about the same. The first day of that battle, 1 July, remains the blackest in the history of the British army, when it suffered 60,000 casualties, of whom more

At his First World War headquarters, Kaiser Wilhelm II discusses tactics with Germany's greatest strategists: Hindenburg (left) and Ludendorff.

The French president Georges Clemenceau (1841–1929) visits the trenches. Clemenceau's personal energy helped to sustain French morale in the face of the horrors of war.

than a third died.

Such figures made nonsense of the confident predictions that the cost of modern war would be bound to make the struggle a short one. This was a reflection of the second surprise, the revelation of the enormous war-making power of industrial societies. Plenty of people were weary by the end of 1916, but by then the warring states had already amply demonstrated a capacity greater than had been imagined to conscript and organize their peoples as never before in history to produce unprecedented quantities of material and furnish the recruits for new armies. Whole societies were engaged against one another; the international solidarity of the working class might never have been thought of for all the resistance it opposed to this, nor the international interests of ruling classes against subversion.

GLOBAL CONFLICT

The inability to batter one another into submission on the battlefields accelerated the strategic and technical expansion of the struggle. This was why diplomats had sought new allies and generals new fronts. The Allies in 1915 mounted an attack on Turkey at the Dardanelles in the hope, not to be realized, of knocking her out of the war and opening up communication with Russia through the Black Sea. The same search for a way round the French deadlock later produced a new Balkan front at Salonika; it replaced the one which had collapsed when Serbia was overrun. Colonial possessions, too, had ensured from the first that there would be fighting all round the globe, even if on a small scale. The German colonies could be picked up fairly easily, thanks to the British command of the

A British tank drags a cannon, seized from the enemy, to the British lines during the Battle of Cambrai in November 1917.

seas, though the African ones provoked some lengthy campaigning. The most important and considerable extra-European operations, though, were in the eastern and southern parts of the Turkish Empire. A British and Indian army entered Mesopotamia. Another force advanced from the Suez Canal towards Palestine. In the Arabian desert, an Arab revolt against the Turks provided some of the few romantic episodes to relieve the brutal squalor of industrial war.

WAR ON A HUGE SCALE

The technical expansion of the war was most noticeable in its industrial effects and in the degeneration of standards of behaviour. The American Civil War a half-century before had prefigured the first of these, too, in revealing the economic demands of mass war in a democratic age. The mills, factories, mines and furnaces of Europe now worked as never before. So did those of the United States and Japan, the former accessible to the Allies but not to the Central Powers because of the British naval supremacy. The maintenance of millions of men in the field required not only arms and ammunition, but food, clothing, medical equipment, and machines in huge quantities. Though a war in which millions of animals were needed, it was also the first war of the internal-combustion engine; trucks and tractors swallowed petrol as avidly as horses and mules ate their fodder. Many statistics illustrate the new scale of war but one must suffice; in 1914 the whole British Empire had 18,000 hospital beds and four years later it had 630,000.

The repercussions of this vast increase in demand rolled outwards through society, leading in all countries in varying measure to the governments' control of the economy, conscription of labour, the revolutionizing of

women's employment, the introduction of new health and welfare services. They also rolled overseas. The United States ceased to be a debtor nation; the Allies liquidated their investments there to pay for what they needed and became debtors in their turn. Indian industry received the fillip it had long required. Boom days came to the ranchers and farmers of the Argentine and the British white Dominions. The latter also shared the military burden, sending soldiers to Europe and fighting the Germans in their colonies.

The British soldier and agent Thomas Edward Lawrence (1888–1935), who become famous as Lawrence of Arabia, played a crucial role in the Arab rebellion against the Ottoman Empire during the First World War. This portrait of Lawrence in Arabian dress was painted in Damascus in 1918.

WHOLE SOCIETIES AS TARGETS

Technical expansion also made the war more frightful. This was not only because machine-guns and high explosive made possible such terrible slaughter. It was not even because of new weapons such as poison gas, flame-throwers or tanks, all of which made their appearance as soldiers strove to find a way out of the deadlock of the battlefield. It was also because the fact that whole societies were engaged in warfare brought with it the real-ization that whole societies could be targets for warlike operations. Attacks on the morale, health and efficiency of civilian work-ers and voters became desirable. When such attacks were denounced, the denunciations were themselves blows in another sort of campaign, that of propaganda. The possibili-ties of mass literacy and the recently created cinema industry supplemented and overtook such old standbys as pulpit and school in this kind of warfare. To British charges that the Germans who carried out primitive bombing raids on London by airship were "baby-killers", Germans retorted that the same could be said of the sailors who sustained the British blockade. The rising figures of German infant mortality bore them out.

BLOCKADES AND THE INVENTION OF SUBMARINES

In part because of the slow but apparently irresistible success of the British blockade and because of its unwillingness to risk the fleet whose building had done so much to poison pre-war feeling between the two countries, the German High Command devised a new use for a weapon whose power had been underrated in 1914, the submarine. It was launched at Allied shipping and the ships of neutrals who were supplying the Allies, attacks often being made without warning and on unarmed vessels. This was first done early in 1915, though few submarines were then available and they did not do much dam-age. There was an outcry when a great British liner was torpedoed that year, with the loss of 1,200 lives, many of them Americans, and the unrestricted sinking of shipping was called off by the Germans. It was resumed at the begin-ning of 1917. By then it was clear that if Germany did not starve Great Britain first, she herself would be choked by British block-ade. During that winter there was famine in Balkan countries and people were starving in the suburbs of Vienna. The French had by then suffered 3,350,000 casualties and the British over a million, the Germans had lost nearly two and a half million and were still fighting a war on two fronts. Food riots and strikes were becoming more frequent; infant mortality was rising towards a level 50 per cent higher than that of 1915. There was no reason to suppose that the German army, divided between east and west, would be any more likely to achieve a knockout than had

At Ypres in 1915 the Germans made the first attempt to use poison gas attacks to break the stalemate. Here, German soldiers are pictured testing gas masks in preparation for an attack.

been the British and French and it was in any case more favourably placed to fight on the defensive. In these circumstances the German general staff chose to resume unrestricted submarine warfare, the decision which brought about the first great transformation of the war in 1917, the entry into it of the United States. The Germans knew this would happen, but gambled on bringing Great Britain to her knees – and thus France – before American weight could be decisive.

THE USA ENTERS THE WAR

American opinion, by no means favourable to one side or the other in 1914, had come a long way since then. Allied propaganda and purchases had helped; so had the first German submarine campaign. When the Allied governments began to talk about war aims which included the reconstruction of Europe on the basis of safeguarding the interests of nationalities it had an appeal to "hyphenated" Americans. The resumption of unrestricted submarine warfare was decisive; it was a direct threat to American interests and the safety of her citizens. When it was also revealed to the American government that Germany hoped to negotiate an alliance with Mexico and Japan against the United States, the hostility aroused by the submarines was confirmed. Soon, an American ship was sunk without warning

These British soldiers in France, blinded by gas in the German offensive of April 1918, are queuing for medical treatment.

inflicted an ineffaceable scar upon the British national consciousness and cost another 400,000 men to gain five miles of mud. Worn out by heroic efforts in 1916, the French army underwent a series of mutinies. Worst of all for the Allies, the Russian empire collapsed and Russia ceased, by the end of the year, to be a great power for the foreseeable future.

THE BOLSHEVIK REVOLUTION

T HE RUSSIAN STATE was destroyed by the war. This was the beginning of the revolutionary transformation of Central and Eastern Europe, too. The makers of what was called a "revolution" in Russia in February 1917 were the German armies which had in the end broken the hearts of even the long-enduring Russian soldiers, who had behind them cities starving because of the breakdown of the transport system and a government of incompetent and corrupt men who feared constitutionalism and liberalism as much as defeat. At the beginning of 1917 the security forces themselves could no longer be depended upon. Food riots were followed by mutiny and the autocracy was suddenly seen to be powerless. A provisional government of liberals and socialists was formed and the tsar abdicated. The new government then itself failed, in the main because it attempted the impossible, the continuation of the war; the Russians wanted peace and bread, as Lenin, the leader of the Bolsheviks, saw. His determination to take power from the moderate provisional government was the second reason for their failure. Presiding over a disintegrating country, administration and army, still facing the unsolved problems of privation in the cities, the provisional government was itself swept away in a second change, the

S ome of the 1,200,000 American soldiers who fought in the First World War are pictured on their way to Europe in autumn 1917. The intervention of the United States played a crucial role in the Allies' victory.

and the United States declared war shortly afterwards.

THE HORRORS OF 1917

The impossibility of breaking the European deadlock by means short of total war had thus sucked the New World into the quarrels of the Old, almost against its will. The Allies were delighted; victory was now assured. Immediately, though, they faced a gloomy year. The year 1917 was even blacker for Great Britain and France than 1916. Not only did the submarine take months to master but a terrible series of battles in France (usually lumped under one name, Passchendaele) coup called the October Revolution which, together with the American entry into the war, marks 1917 as a break between two eras of European history. Previously, Europe had settled its own affairs; now the United States would be bound to have a large say in its future and there had come into being a state which was committed by the beliefs of its founders to the destruction of the whole pre-war European order, a truly and consciously revolutionary centre for world politics.

RUSSIA LEAVES THE WAR

The immediate and obvious consequence of the establishment of the Union of Soviet Socialist Republics (USSR), as Russia was now called, after the workers' and soldiers' councils which were her basic political institution after the revolution, was a new strategic situation. The Bolsheviks consolidated their *coup d'état* by dissolving (since they did not control it) the only freely elected representative body based on universal suffrage Russia ever had and by trying to secure the peasant's loyalties by promises of land and peace. This was essential if they were to survive; the backbone of the party which now strove to assert its authority over Russia was the very small industrial working class of a few cities. Only peace could provide a safer and broader foundation. At first the terms demanded by the Germans were thought so

This contemporary painting shows Vladimir Ilyich Lenin (1870–1924) addressing the crowds in Petrograd in 1920. The Bolshevik leader's determination and energy were central to his party's ability to cling to power in the chaos that followed the October Revolution. Large areas of Russia had been devastated by the war.

German and Russian representatives are depicted at the preliminary peace negotiations held in Brest-Litovsk in December 1917. Trotsky deliberately prolonged the talks, hoping that the proletarian revolution would spread throughout Europe. The failure of this revolution to materialize and the revival of the German advance through her territory in February eventually forced the Soviet Union to accept Germany's harsh conditions.

Leon Trotsky (1879–1940) was the Soviet commissar of war from the beginning of 1918 and founded the Red Army. Here he is shown haranguing his troops during the Civil War of 1918–1921.

objectionable that the Russians stopped negotiation; they then had to accept a much more punitive outcome, the Treaty of Brest-Litovsk, in March 1918. It imposed severe losses of territory, but gave the new order the peace and time it desperately needed to tackle its internal troubles.

ALLIED HOSTILITY TO RUSSIA

The Allies were furious with the Bolsheviks, whose action they saw as a treacherous defection. Nor was their attitude towards the new régime softened by the intransigent revolutionary propaganda it directed against their citizens. The Russian leaders expected a revolution of the working class in all the advanced capitalist countries. This gave an extra dimension to a series of military interventions in the affairs of Russia by the Allies.

Their original purpose was strategic, in that they hoped to stop the Germans exploiting the advantage of being able to close down their eastern front, but they were quickly interpreted by many people in the capitalist countries and by all Bolsheviks as anti-communist crusades. Worse still, they became entangled in a civil war which seemed likely to destroy the new régime. Even without the doctrinal filter of Marxist theory through which Lenin and his colleagues saw the world, these episodes would have been likely to sour relations between Russia and the capitalist countries for a long time; once translated into Marxist terms they seemed a confirmation of an essential and ineradicable hostility. Their recollection has dogged Russian attitudes ever since. They also helped to justify the Russian revolution's turn downwards into authoritarian government. Fear of the invader as a restorer of the old order and patron of landlords combined with Russian traditions of autocracy and police terrorism to stifle any liberalization of the régime.

THE EXPLOITATION OF NATIONALISM

The Russian communists' conviction that revolution was about to occur in Central and Western Europe was in one sense correct, yet crucially wrong. In its last year, war's revolutionary potential indeed became plain, but in national, not class, forms. The Allies were provoked (in part by the Bolsheviks) to a revolution strategy of their own. The military situation looked bleak for them at the end of 1917. It was obvious that they would face a German attack in France in the spring without the advantage of a Russian army to draw off their enemies and that it would be a long time before American troops arrived in large numbers to help them in France. But they

General Kornilov, the Cossack commander-in-chief of the Russian army, is seen here reviewing his troops. He led a muddled *coup d'état* in the summer of 1917 and was later one of the main organizers of the first White Army which confronted the Bolsheviks. He died in combat at the beginning of the Civil War.

could adopt a revolutionary weapon. They could appeal to the nationalities of the Austro-Hungarian Empire. This had the additional advantage of emphasizing in American eyes the ideological purity of the Allied cause now that it was no longer tied to tsardom. Accordingly, in 1918, subversive propaganda was directed at the Austro-Hungarian armies and encouragement was given to Czechs and South Slavs in exile. Before Germany gave in, the Dual Monarchy was already dissolving under the combined effects of reawakened national sentiment and a Balkan campaign which at last began to provide victories. This was the second great blow to old Europe. The political structure of the whole area bounded by the Urals, the Baltic and the Danube valley was now in question as it had not been for centuries. There was even a Polish army again in existence. It was patronized by the Germans as a weapon against Russia, while the American president announced that an independent Poland was an essential of Allied peacemaking. All the certainties of the past century seemed to be in the melting-pot.

THE PRICE OF WAR

The crucial battles were fought against an increasingly revolutionary background. By the summer, the Allies had managed to halt the last great German offensive. It had made huge gains, but not enough. When the Allied armies began to move forward victoriously in their turn, the German leaders sought an end: they, too, thought they saw signs of revolutionary collapse at home. When the kaiser abdicated, the third of the dynastic empires had fallen; the Habsburgs had already gone, so that the Hohenzollerns just outlasted their old rivals. A new German government requested an armistice and the fighting came to an end.

The cost of this huge conflict has never been adequately computed. One figure which is approximate indicates its scale: about ten million men had died as a result of direct military action. Yet typhus probably killed another million in the Balkans alone. Even such horrible figures as these do not indicate the physical cost in maiming, blinding, the loss to families of fathers and husbands, the spiritual havoc in the destruction of ideals, confidence and goodwill. Europeans looked at their huge cemeteries and were appalled at what they had done. The economic damage was immense, too. Over much of Europe people starved. A year after the war manufacturing output was still nearly a quarter below that of 1914; Russia's was only 20 per cent of what it had then been. Transport was in some countries almost impossible to procure. Moreover all the complicated, fragile machinery of international exchange was smashed and some of it could never be replaced. At the centre of this chaos lay, exhausted, a Germany which had been the economic dynamo of Central Europe. "We are at the dead season of our fortunes," wrote J.M. Keynes, a young British economist at the peace conference. "Our power of feeling or caring beyond the immediate questions of our own material well-being is temporarily eclipsed ... We have been moved beyond endurance, and need rest. Never in the lifetime of men now living has the universal element in the soul of man burnt so dimly."

THE PEACE

DELEGATES TO A PEACE CONFERENCE began to assemble at the end of 1918. It was once the fashion to emphasize their failures, but perspective and the recognition of the magnitude of their tasks imposes a certain respect for what they did. It was the greatest settlement since 1815 and its authors had to reconcile great expectations with stubborn facts. The power to make the crucial decisions was remarkably concentrated: the British and French prime ministers and the American president, Woodrow Wilson, dominated the negotiations. These took place between the victors; the defeated Germans were subsequently presented with their terms. In the diverging interests of France, aware above all of the appalling danger of any third repetition of German aggression, and of the Anglo-Saxon nations, conscious of standing in no such peril, lay the central problem of European security, but many others surrounded and obscured it. The peace settlement had to be a world settlement. It not only dealt with territories outside Europe – as earlier great settlements had done – but many non-European voices were heard in its making. Of twenty-seven states whose representatives signed the main treaty, a majority, seventeen, lay in other continents. The United States was the greatest of these; with Japan, Great Britain, France and Italy she formed the group described as the "principal" victorious powers. For a world settlement, nevertheless,

Crowds watch the Victory Parade in Paris in 1919. The satisfaction of victory did not last long in France, where the fear of possible retribution by Germany surfaced a few years later.

enemies with whom peace had to be made. All of this posed difficult problems. But the main concern of the Peace Conference was the settlement with Germany embodied in the Treaty of Versailles signed in June 1919.

THE TREATY OF VERSAILLES

The Treaty of Versailles was a punitive settlement and explicitly stated that the Germans were responsible for the outbreak of war. But most of the harshest terms arose not from this moral guilt but from the French wish, if possible, so to tie Germany down that any third German war was inconceivable. This was the purpose of economic reparations, which were the most unsatisfactory part of the settlement. They angered Germans and made acceptance of defeat even harder. Moreover they were economic nonsense. Nor was the penalizing of Germany supported by arrangements to ensure that Germany might not one day try to reverse the decision by force of arms, and this angered the French. Germany's territorial losses, it went without saying, included Alsace and Lorraine, but were otherwise greatest in the east, to Poland. In the west the French did not get much more reassurance than an undertaking that the German bank of the Rhine should be "demilitarized".

Guards watch over German prisoners-of-war in a French camp at the end of the First World War.

it was ominous that no representative attended from Russia, the only great power with both European and Asian frontiers.

Technically, the peace settlement consisted of a group of distinct treaties made not only with Germany, but Bulgaria, Turkey and the "succession states" which claimed the divided Dual Monarchy. Of these a resurrected Poland, an enlarged Serbia called Yugoslavia and an entirely new Czechoslovakia were present at the conference as allies, while a much reduced Hungary and the Germanic heart of old Austria were treated as defeated

The last page of the Treaty of Versailles contains the signatures and seals of the delegates of the United States, headed by President Wilson.

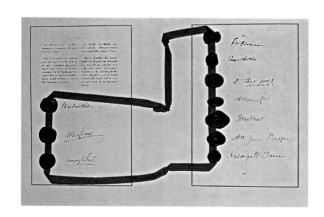

PROBLEMS OF NATIONALITY

The second leading characteristic of the peace was its attempt where possible to follow the principles of self-determination and nationality. In many places this merely meant recognizing existing facts; Poland and Czechoslovakia were already in existence as states before the peace conference met, and Yugoslavia was built round the core of the

The signing of the peace in the Hall of Mirrors in Versailles (28 June, 1919) is depicted in this famous painting by Sir William Orpen (1878–1931).

former Serbia. By the end of 1918, therefore, these principles had already triumphed over much of the area occupied by the old Dual Monarchy (and were soon to do so also in the former Baltic provinces of Russia). After outlasting even the Holy Roman Empire, the Habsburgs were gone at last and in their place appeared states which, though not uninterruptedly, were to survive most of the rest of the century. The principle of self-determination was also followed in providing that certain frontier zones should have their destiny settled by plebiscite.

Unfortunately, the principle of nationality

The Romanian royal family sits for a photograph at home in 1922. Romania, which had fought on the Allies' side during the war and had seen great tracts of its land occupied by the enemy, was treated favourably in the Paris peace treaty. It was allowed to annex the vast and ethnically diverse region of Transylvania, which had previously belonged to Hungary.

could not always be applied. Geographical, historical, cultural and economic realities cut across it. When it prevailed over them – as in the destruction of the Danube's economic unity – the results could be bad; when it did not they could be just as bad because of the aggrieved feelings left behind. Eastern and Central Europe were studded with national minorities embedded resentfully in nations to which they felt no allegiance. A third of Poland's population did not speak Polish; more than a third of Czechoslovakia's consisted of minorities of Poles, Russians, Germans, Magyars and Ruthenes; an enlarged Romania now contained over a million Magyars. In some places, the infringement of the principle was felt with especial acuteness as an injustice. Germans resented the existence of a "corridor" connecting Poland with the sea across German lands, Italy was disappointed of Adriatic spoils held out to her by her allies when they had needed her help, and the Irish had still not got Home Rule after all.

THE LEAGUE OF NATIONS

The most obvious non-European question concerned the disposition of the German colonies. Here there was an important innovation. Old-fashioned colonial greed was not acceptable to the United States; instead, tutelage for non-European peoples formerly under German or Turkish rule was provided by the device of trusteeship. "Mandates" were given to the victorious powers (though the United States declined any) by a new "League of Nations" to administer these territories while they were prepared for self-government; it was the most imaginative idea to emerge from the settlement, even though it was used to drape with respectability the last major conquests of European imperialism.

The League of Nations owed much to the enthusiasm of the American president, Woodrow Wilson, who ensured its Covenant – its constitution – pride of place as the first part of the Peace Treaty. It was the one instance in which the settlement transcended the idea of nationalism (even the British Empire had been represented as individual units, one of which, significantly, was India). It also transcended that of Europe; it is another sign of the new era that twenty-six of the original forty-two members of the League were countries outside Europe. Unfortunately, because of domestic politics Wilson had not taken into account, the United States was not among them. This was the most fatal of several grave weaknesses which made it impossible for the League to satisfy the expectations it had aroused. Perhaps these were all unrealizable in principle, given the actual state of world political forces. None the less, the League was to have its successes in handling matters which might without its intervention have proved dangerous. If exaggerated hopes had been entertained that it might do more, it does not mean it was not a practical as well as a great and imaginative idea.

RUSSIA'S ABSENCE FROM THE PEACE CONFERENCE

Russia was absent from the League just as she was from the peace conference. Probably the latter was the more important. The political

---

The League of Nations

On 28th April, 1919, the delegates of the Paris peace conference signed the pact of the League of Nations, which took effect in January 1920. The League's objective was to "promote international cooperation and to achieve international peace and security".

From the start, the League of Nations was disadvantaged by the absence of the United States. Also, neither the countries defeated in the First World War nor Soviet Russia were members. The Soviet Union joined in 1934. Germany joined in 1926, but in 1933 Hitler withdrew its membership and his gesture was copied by Mussolini for Italy in 1937. Japan had also withdrawn in 1933. This meant that there were always important absentees.

The League of Nations had its seat in Geneva. It was made up of the General Assembly, comprised of all the member nations; the Council, made up of four permanent members (Great Britain, France, Italy and Japan) and others elected for three-year periods; and the Secretariat, which prepared agendas and reports. The League's powers were limited: unable to decree military interventions, it could only oppose aggression with economic sanctions. Its subsidiary bodies included the International Labour Organization, which campaigned for governments to pass legislation on minimum wages and maximum working hours.

In spite of its restrictions, the League sometimes succeeded in averting international conflict: in 1921, for example, when Yugoslavia invaded Albania, and in 1925, when Bulgaria invaded Greece. Its failure to have any effect, however, when Japan invaded Manchuria in 1931, and when Italy invaded Ethiopia in 1935, led Great Britain and France to reject suggestions that it could be used against Nazi Germany. During the Second World War, the idea of replacing the League with a more effective organization dominated discussion and eventually gave rise to the United Nations.

The driving force behind the League of Nations was the United States president Woodrow Wilson (1856–1924).

arrangements to shape the next stage of European history were entered into without consulting her, though in Eastern Europe this meant the drawing of boundaries in which any Russian government was bound to be vitally interested. It was true that the Bolshevik leaders did all they could to provide excuses for excluding them. They envenomed relations with the major powers by revolutionary propaganda, for they were convinced that the capitalist countries were determined to overthrow them. The British prime minister, Lloyd George, and Wilson were in fact more flexible – even sympathetic – than many of their colleagues and electors in dealing with Russia. Their French colleague, Clemenceau, on the other hand, was passionately anti-Bolshevik and had the support of many French ex-soldiers and investors in being so; Versailles was the first great European peace to be made by powers all the time aware of the dangers of disappointing democratic electorates. But however the responsibility is allocated, the outcome was that Russia, the European power which had, potentially, the greatest weight of all in the affairs of the continent, was not consulted in the making of a new Europe. Though for the time being virtually out of action, she was bound eventually to join the ranks of those who wished to revise the settlement or overthrow it. It only made it worse that her rulers detested the social system it was meant to protect.

THE WEAKNESSES OF THE PEACE

Huge hopes had been entertained of the peace settlement. They were often unrealistic, yet in spite of its manifest failures, the peace has been over-condemned, for it had many good

The new Irish Free State was plagued by a civil war (1922–1923) between the provisional government and the Irregulars, who opposed the terms of the Anglo-Irish Treaty. Members of the Irish Republican Army (the armed wing of those who opposed the treaty) can be seen here marching through the streets during the Dublin Battle of July 1922.

points. When it failed, it was for reasons which were for the most part beyond the control of the men who made it. In the first place, the days of a European world hegemony in the narrow political sense were over. The peace treaties of 1919 could do little to secure the future beyond Europe. The old imperial policemen were now too weakened to do their job inside Europe, let alone outside; some had disappeared altogether. In the end the United States had been needed to ensure Germany's defeat but now she plunged into a period of artificial isolation. Nor did Russia wish to be involved in the continent's stabilizing. The isolationism of the one power and the sterilization of the other by ideology left Europe to its own inadequate devices. When no revolution broke out in Europe, the Russians turned in on themselves; when Americans were given the chance by Wilson to be involved in Europe's peace-keeping, they refused it. Both decisions are comprehensible, but their combined effect was to preserve an illusion of European autonomy which was no longer a reality and could no longer be an adequate framework for handling its problems. Finally, the settlement's gravest immediate weakness lay in the economic fragility of the new structures it presupposed. Here its terms were more in question: self-determination often made nonsense of economics. But it is difficult to see on what grounds self-determination could have been set aside. Ireland's problems are still with us more than a half-century after an independent Irish Free State appeared in 1922.

ILLUSIONS OF SUCCESS

The situation was all the more likely to prove unstable because many illusions persisted in Europe and many new ones arose. Allied victory and the rhetoric of peace-making made many think that there had been a great triumph of liberalism and democracy. Four autocratic anti-national illiberal empires had collapsed, after all, and to this day the peace settlement retains the distinction of being the only one in history made by great powers all of whom were democracies. Liberal optimism also drew strength from the ostentatious stance taken by Wilson during the war; he had done all he could to make it clear that he saw the participation of the United States as essentially different in kind from that of the other Allies, being governed (he reiterated) by high-minded ideals and a belief that the world could be made safe for democracy if other nations would give up their bad old ways. Some thought that he had been shown to be right; the new states, above all the new Germany, adopted liberal, parliamentary constitutions and often republican ones, too. Finally, there was the illusion of the League; the dream of a new international authority which was not an empire seemed at last a reality.

This British cartoon, dating from 1927, mocks Communist propaganda. The speaker, who does not look as proletarian as the sparse public he is addressing, is surrounded by posters bearing slogans such as "Against King and Country!" and "Up the Reds!".

EUROPE'S FEAR OF COMMUNIST REVOLUTION

IDEAS OF THE PEACE SETTLEMENT as a triumph of liberalism and democracy were rooted in fallacy and false premise. Since the peace-makers had been obliged to do much more than enthrone liberal principles – they had also to pay debts, protect vested interests, and take account of intractable facts – those principles had been much muddied in practice. Above all, they had left much unsatisfied nationalism about and had created new and fierce nationalist resentments in Germany. Perhaps this could not be helped, but it was a soil in which things other than liberalism could grow. Further, the democratic institutions of the new states – and the old ones, too, for that matter – were being launched on a world whose economic structure was terribly damaged. Everywhere, poverty, hardship and unemployment exacerbated political struggle and in many places they were made worse by the special dislocations produced by respect for national sovereignty. The crumbling of old economic patterns of exchange in the war made it much more difficult to deal with problems like peasant poverty and unemployment, too; Russia, once the granary of much of Western Europe, was now

Communism

Proposals for the organization of social life based on collective property have been made from ancient times. Although he was far from being a communist philosopher, Plato, in the 4th century BCE, maintained that in an ideal state the ruling class should have neither property nor family. In the 16th century, the Englishman Thomas More described for the first time, in his book *Utopia*, an imaginary society where not just a minority but all its members shared collective property. During the French Revolution Gracchus Babeuf proposed the establishment of a communist society through a revolutionary conspiracy.

Modern communism emerged with the *Communist Manifesto* (1848) of Karl Marx and Friedrich Engels. According to Marx, history was leading inevitably towards the establishment of a communist society, in which the disappearance of private property and state structures would make people completely free. Lenin's dream of creating a society in which he could put Marx's theories into practice was realized when the Bolsheviks seized power in Russia in 1917. The following year, the Bolshevik Party became the Communist Party, and in 1919 the Communist International, or Comintern, was founded. However, by the time the Communist Party lost power in Russia in 1991, the countries ruled by Communist governments were more characterized by an immense state bureaucracy than by the "withering away" of the state envisaged by Marx.

Vladimir Ilyich Lenin (left), founder of the Soviet Union and of the international Communist movement, is photographed with his successor, Joseph Stalin.

inaccessible economically. This was a background which revolutionaries could exploit. The Communists were happy and ready to do this, for they believed that history had cast them for this role, and soon their efforts were reinforced in some countries by another radical phenomenon, Fascism.

INTERNATIONAL COMMUNISM

Communism threatened the new Europe in two ways. Internally, each country soon had a revolutionary communist party. They effected little that was positive, but caused great alarm. They also did much to prevent the emergence of strong progressive parties. This was because of the circumstances of their birth. A "Comintern", or Third International, was devised by the Russians in March 1919 to provide leadership for the international socialist movement which might otherwise, they feared, rally again to the old leaders whose lack of revolutionary zeal they blamed for a failure to exploit the opportunities of the war. The test of socialist movements for Lenin was adherence to the Comintern, whose principles were deliberately rigid, disciplined and uncompromising, in accordance with his view of the needs of an effective revolutionary party. In almost every country this divided socialists into two camps. Some adhered to the Comintern and took the name Communist; others, though sometimes claiming still to be Marxists, remained in the rump national parties and movements. They competed for working-class support and fought one another bitterly.

The new revolutionary threat on the Left was all the more alarming to many Europeans because there were plenty of revolutionary possibilities for Communists to exploit. The most conspicuous led to the installation of a Bolshevik government in Hungary, but more

Russia during the First World War

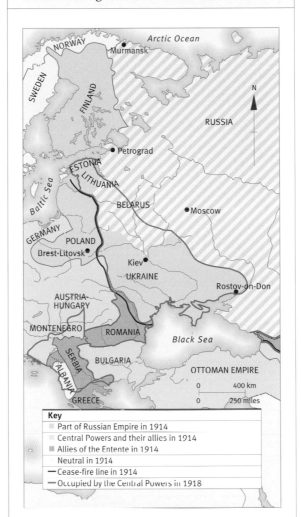

Key
- Part of Russian Empire in 1914
- Central Powers and their allies in 1914
- Allies of the Entente in 1914
- Neutral in 1914
- Cease-fire line in 1914
- Occupied by the Central Powers in 1918

When the Russian Communist government signed the Brest-Litovsk Peace Treaty with the Central Powers in March 1918, the latter had occupied a vast territory on the western fronts of the old tsarist empire. As a result of the defeat of Germany, the Communists regained the Ukraine and Belarus which, in 1922, were integrated into the Union of Soviet Socialist Republics together with Russia and Transcaucasia. Finland, the three Baltic states and Poland, on the other hand, consolidated their independence.

startling, perhaps, were attempted Communist coups in Germany, some briefly successful. The German situation was especially ironical, for the government of the new republic which emerged there in the aftermath of defeat was dominated by socialists who were forced back to reliance upon conservative forces – notably the professional soldiers of the old army – in order to prevent revolution. This happened even before the founding of the Comintern and it gave a special bitterness to the divisions of the Left in Germany. But everywhere, Communist policy made united resistance to conservatism more difficult, frightening moderates with revolutionary rhetoric and conspiracy.

FEAR OF RUSSIA IN EASTERN EUROPE

In Eastern Europe, the social threat was often seen also as a Russian threat. The Comintern was manipulated as an instrument of Soviet foreign policy by the Bolshevik leaders; this was justifiable, given their assumption that the future of world revolution depended upon the preservation of the first socialist state as a citadel of the international working class. In the early years of civil war and slow consolidation of Bolshevik power in Russia that belief led to the deliberate incitement of disaffection abroad in order to preoccupy capitalist governments. But in Eastern and Central Europe there was more to it than this, because the actual territorial settlement of that area was in doubt long after the Versailles treaty. The First World War did not end there until in March 1921 a peace treaty between Russia and the new Polish Republic provided frontiers lasting until 1939. Poland was the most anti-Russian by tradition, the most anti-Bolshevik by religion, as well as the largest and most ambitious of the new nations. But all of them felt threatened by a recovery of Russian power, especially now that it was tied up with the threat of social revolution. This connexion helped to turn many of these states before 1939 to dictator-

Proletarian dictatorship

Lenin defined the new Russian régime as a proletarian dictatorship, but it soon became clear that it was a dictatorship not by the working masses, but by a centralized and disciplined party.

"The dictatorship of the proletariat means a most determined and most ruthless war waged by the new class against a more powerful enemy, the bourgeoisie, whose resistance is increased tenfold by their overthrow (even if only in a single country), and whose power lies, not only in the strength of international capital, the strength and durability of their international connections, but also in the force of habit, in the strength of small-scale production. Unfortunately, small-scale production is still widespread in the world, and small-scale production engenders capitalism and the bourgeoisie continuously, daily, hourly, spontaneously, and on a mass scale. All these reasons make the dictatorship of the proletariat necessary, and victory over the bourgeoisie is impossible without a long, stubborn and desperate life-and-death struggle which calls for tenacity, discipline and a single and inflexible will."

An extract from Ch. 2 of 'Left-Wing' Communism: an infantile disorder by Vladimir Ilyich Lenin (1920).

ial or military governments which would at least guarantee a strong anti-Communist line.

POST-REVOLUTIONARY RUSSIA

FEAR OF COMMUNIST REVOLUTION in Eastern and Central Europe was most evident in the immediate post-war years, when economic collapse and uncertainty about the outcome of the Polish-Russian war (which, at one time, appeared to threaten Warsaw itself) provided the background. In 1921, with

In the aftermath of the First World War, the October Revolution and the Civil War, famine inflicted further misery on millions of Russians, such as this family of starving peasants.

peace at last and, symbolically, the establishment of orderly official relations between the USSR and Great Britain, there was a noticeable relaxation. This was connected with the Russian government's own sense of emerging from a period of acute danger in the civil war. It did not produce much in the way of better diplomatic manners, and revolutionary propaganda and denunciation of capitalist countries did not cease, but the Bolsheviks could now turn to the rebuilding of their own shattered land. In 1921 Russian pig-iron production was about one-fifth of its 1913 level, that of coal a tiny 3 per cent or so, while the railways had less than half as many locomotives in service as at the start of the war. Livestock had declined by over a quarter and cereal deliveries were less than two-fifths of those of 1916. On to this impoverished economy there fell in 1921 a drought in south Russia. More than two million died in the subsequent famine and even cannibalism was reported.

INTERNAL POLITICAL STRIFE

Liberalization of the economy brought about a turnround. By 1927 both industrial and agricultural production were nearly back to pre-war levels. The régime in these years was undergoing great uncertainty in its leadership. This had already been apparent before Lenin died in 1924, but the removal of a man whose acknowledged ascendancy had kept forces within it in balance opened a period of evolution and debate in the leadership of the Communist Party. This was not about the centralized, autocratic nature of the régime which had emerged from the 1917 revolution, for none of the protagonists considered that political liberation was conceivable or that the use of secret police and the party's dictatorship could be dispensed with in a world of hostile capitalist states. But they could disagree about economic policy and tactics and personal rivalry sometimes gave extra edge to this.

Broadly speaking, two viewpoints emerged. One emphasized that the revolution depended on the goodwill of the mass of Russians, the peasants; they had first been allowed to take the land, then antagonized by attempts to feed the cities at their expense, then conciliated again by the liberalization of the economy and what was known as "NEP", the New Economic Policy which Lenin had approved as an expedient. Under it, the peasants had been able to make profits for themselves and had begun to grow more food and to sell it to the cities. The other viewpoint

showed the same facts in a longer perspective. To conciliate the peasants would slow down industrialization, which Russia needed to survive in a hostile world. The Party's proper course, argued those who took this view, was to rely upon the revolutionary militants of the cities and to exploit the still non-Bolshevized peasants in their interest while pressing on with industrialization and the promotion of revolution abroad. The Communist leader Trotsky took this view.

STALIN AND INDUSTRIALIZATION

What happened was roughly that Trotsky was shouldered aside, but his view prevailed. From the intricate politics of the Party there emerged eventually the ascendancy of a

This painting by Yuri Pimenov is entitled *New Moscow* and gives an unusually light-hearted impression of life in the Soviet Union under Stalin. In fact the 1930s brought the imprisonment or execution of millions of Soviet citizens, many of them veteran Communists, in Stalin's so-called purges.

Joseph Stalin, sitting fifth from the left in the front row, is pictured among the delegates of the 8th Congress of the Soviets in 1936. On the left of the front row is Nikita Khruschev, who would denounce Stalin's crimes 20 years later. At the other end of the row is Marshal Mikhail Tukhachevsky, who became a victim of the purges in 1937.

member of its bureaucracy, Joseph Stalin, a man far less attractive intellectually than either Lenin or Trotsky, equally ruthless, and of greater historical importance. Gradually arming himself with a power which he used against former colleagues and old Bolsheviks as willingly as against his enemies, he carried out the real Russian revolution to which the Bolshevik seizure of power had opened the way and created a new élite on which a new Russia was to be based. For him industrialization was paramount. The road to it lay through finding a way of forcing the peasant to pay for it by supplying the grain he would rather have eaten if not offered a good profit. Two "Five Year Plans" carried out an industrialization programme from 1928 onwards, and their roots lay in the collectivization of agriculture. The Party now for the first time conquered the countryside. In a new civil war millions of peasants were killed or transported, and grain levies brought back famine. But the towns were fed, though the police apparatus kept consumption down to the minimum. There was a fall in real wages. But by 1937 80 per cent of Russian industrial output came from plant built since 1928. Russia was again a great power and the effects of this alone would assure Stalin a place in history.

The price in suffering was enormous. The enforcement of collectivization was only made possible by brutality on a scale far greater than anything seen under the tsars and it made Russia a totalitarian state far more effective than the old autocracy had been. Stalin, though himself a Georgian, looks a fully Russian figure, a despot whose ruthless use of power is anticipated by an Ivan the Terrible or a Peter the Great. He was also a somewhat paradoxical claimant to Marxist orthodoxy, which taught that the economic structure of society determined its politics. Stalin precisely inverted this; he demonstrated that if the will to use political power was there, the economic substructure could be revolutionized by force.

ITALIAN FASCISM

CRITICS OF LIBERAL CAPITALIST society in other countries often held up Soviet Russia, of which they had a very rosy picture, as an example of the way in which a society might achieve progress and a revitalization of its cultural and ethical life. But this was not the only model offered to those who found the civilization of the West disappointing. In

the 1920s in Italy a movement appeared called Fascism. It was to lend its name to a number of other and only loosely related radical movements in other countries which had in common a rejection of liberalism and strong anti-Marxism. The Great War had badly strained constitutional Italy. Though poorer than other countries regarded in 1914 as great powers, her share of fighting had been disproportionately heavy and often unsuccessful and much of it had taken place on Italian territory. Inequalities had accentuated social divisions as the war went on. With peace came even faster inflation, too. The owners of property, whether agricultural or industrial, and those who could ask higher

Fascism in Italy and Germany

Fascism was a political movement founded in Italy by Benito Mussolini in 1919. It greatly changed Europe during the period between the wars, when several other political parties, influenced by the Italian Fascist example, were established, including the German National Socialist Party. The Italian Fascists and similar parties in other countries claimed to be against all the other political movements then in existence. They were anti-liberal and anti-socialist, fiercely anti-Communist and to a certain degree, anti-conservative, although in many cases they allied themselves with the conservative right-wing parties.

The objective of the Italian and German Fascists was to establish nationalist, authoritarian states, which would intervene in economic, social and cultural affairs. They aspired to territorial expansion through conflict. They were aggressive and secular; they glorified youth, masculinity and war, and paid homage to charismatic leaders with carefully manipulated cults of personality.

Germany and Italy's defeat in the Second World War – and the memory of the atrocities committed by their Fascist régimes – completely undermined any prestige the doctrine had acquired in the pre-war era. However, neo-Fascist movements have recently emerged in several European countries, often as a result of rising levels of youth unemployment.

Benito Mussolini (1883–1945) (left) is pictured with the writer Gabriele d'Annunzio, who actively promoted ultra-nationalistic attitudes at the end of the First World War.

wages because of a labour shortage, were more insulated against it than the middle classes and those who lived on investment or fixed incomes. Yet these were on the whole the most convinced supporters of the unification completed in 1870. They had sustained a constitutional and liberal state while conservative Roman Catholics and revolutionary socialists had long opposed it. They had seen the war Italy entered in 1915 as an extension of the Risorgimento, the nineteenth-century struggle to unite Italy as a nation, a crusade to remove Austria from the last soil she ruled which was inhabited by those of Italian blood or speech. Like all nationalism, this was a muddled, unscientific notion, but it was powerful.

Peace brought to Italians disappointment and disillusion; many nationalist dreams were left unrealized. Moreover, as the immediate post-war economic crisis deepened, the socialists grew stronger in parliament and seemed more alarming now that a socialist revolutionary state existed in Russia. Disappointed and frightened, tired of socialist anti-nationalism, many Italians began to cast loose from liberal parliamentarianism and to look for a way out of Italy's disappointments. They were sympathetic to intransigent nationalism abroad (for example, to an adventurer who seized the Adriatic port of Fiume which the Peace Conference had failed to give to Italy) and violent anti-Marxism at home. The second was bound to be attractive in a Roman Catholic country, but it was not only from the traditionally conservative Church that the new leadership against Marxism came.

BENITO MUSSOLINI

In 1919 a journalist and ex-serviceman who had before the war been an extreme socialist,

Mussolini is depicted at the head of the Fascist militia in an idealized portrayal of the "March on Rome" of 1922. In reality, Mussolini did not march on Rome at all, but travelled by train in comfort, arriving before his followers.

Benito Mussolini, formed a movement called the *fascio di combattimento*, which can be roughly translated as "union for struggle". It sought power by any means, among them violence by groups of young thugs, directed at first against socialists and working-class organizations, then against elected authorities. The movement prospered. Italy's constitutional politicians could neither control it nor tame it by cooperation. Soon the Fascists (as they came to be called) often enjoyed official or quasi-official patronage and protection from local officials and police. Gangsterism was semi-institutionalized. By 1922 they had not only achieved important electoral success but had virtually made orderly government impossible in some places by terrorizing their political enemies, especially if they were communist or socialist. In that year, other politicians having failed to master the Fascist challenge, the king called Mussolini to form a government; he did so, on a coalition basis, and the violence came to an end. This was what was called in later

Fascist mythology the "March on Rome", but was not quite the end of constitutional Italy. Mussolini only slowly turned his position into a dictatorship. In 1926 government by decree began; elections were suspended. There was little opposition.

FASCIST GOVERNMENT

The new régime had terrorism in plenty at its roots, and it explicitly denounced liberal ideals, yet Mussolini's rule was far short of totalitarian and was much less brutal than the Russian (of which he sometimes spoke admiringly). He undoubtedly had aspirations to revolutionary change, and many of his followers much stronger ones, but revolution turned out in practice to be largely a propaganda claim; Mussolini's own temperamental impatience with an established society from which he felt excluded lay behind it, as much as real radical pressure in his movement. Italian Fascism in practice and theory rarely achieved coherence; instead, it reflected more and more the power of established Italy. Its greatest domestic step was a diplomatic agreement with the papacy, which in return

Cardinal Gasbarri signs the Lateran treaties in 1929, while Mussolini (seated on right) looks on.

Mussolini's Fascist doctrines

"Above all, Fascism ... does not believe in the possibility nor the usefulness of perpetual peace ... . Only war takes all human energy to its maximum pressure and stamps the seal of nobility on those peoples who have the courage to confront it ... .

"This conception of life makes Fascism totally opposed to the doctrine, based on so-called scientific and Marxist socialism, which is the materialist concept of history. ... Fascism, now and always, believes in sanctity and heroism; that is to say, in actions which are not influenced by direct or indirect economic motives. ... Fascism denies the validity of the equation welfare equals happiness, which would reduce men to the level of animals ... .

"As well as socialism, Fascism fights the whole complex system of democratic ideology ... . Fascism refuses to accept that the majority, by the simple fact of being a majority, can lead human society ... and affirms the immutable, beneficial and advantageous inequality of humankind ... .

"The basis of Fascism is its concept of state. Fascism sees the state as an absolute, compared to which all individuals or groups are relative ... .

An extract from *Fascist Doctrines* by Benito Mussolini, 1932.

for substantial concessions to the authority of the Church in Italian life (which persist to this day) recognized the Italian state officially for the first time. For all Fascism's revolutionary rhetoric, the Lateran treaties of 1929 which embodied this agreement were a concession to the greatest conservative force in Italy. "We have given back God to Italy and Italy to God," said the pope. Just as unrevolutionary were the results of Fascist criticism of free enterprise. The subordination of individual interest to the state boiled down to depriving trades unions of their power to protect their members' interests. Few checks were placed on the freedom of employers and Fascist economic planning was a mockery. Only agricultural production notably improved.

AUTHORITARIANISM ELSEWHERE IN EUROPE

The same divergence between style and aspiration on the one hand and achievement on the other was also to be marked in movements elsewhere which have been called Fascist. Though indeed reflecting something new and post-liberal – they were inconceivable except as expressions of mass society – such movements almost always in practice made compromising concessions to conservative influences. This makes it difficult to speak of the phenomenon "Fascism" at all precisely; in many countries régimes appeared which were authoritarian – even totalitarian in aspiration – intensely nationalist, and anti-Marxist. But Fascism was not the only possible source of such ideas. Such governments as those which emerged in Portugal and Spain, for example, drew upon traditional and conservative forces rather than upon those which arose from the new phenomenon of mass politics. In them, true radicals who were Fascists often felt discontented at concessions made to the existing social order. Only in Germany, in the end, did a movement some termed "Fascist" succeed in a revolution which mastered historical conservatism. For such reasons, the label of Fascism sometimes confuses as much as it clarifies.

DEMOCRACY THWARTED

Perhaps it is best merely to distinguish two separable phenomena of the twenty years after 1918. One is the appearance (even in stable democracies such as Great Britain and

France) of ideologists and activists who spoke the language of a new, radical politics, emphasized idealism, will-power and sacrifice, and looked forward to rebuilding society and the state on new lines without respect to vested interests or concessions to materialism. This was a phenomenon which, though widespread, triumphed in only two major states, Italy and Germany. In each of these, economic collapse, outraged nationalism and anti-Marxism were the sources of success, though that in Germany did not come until 1933. If one word is wanted for this, let it be

Mussolini is accompanied by top military aides. The Fascist leader's decision to take part in the Second World War was fatal both for him and for his régime.

Admiral Miklos Horthy (1868–1957) was head of state in Hungary from 1920 until 1944, having commanded the troops which overthrew Béla Kun's Communist régime in 1919. Horthy's was one of many conservative dictatorships that were established in Europe in the period between the wars.

Fascism. In other countries, usually under-developed economically, it might be better to speak of authoritarian, rather than Fascist, régimes, especially in Eastern Europe. There, large agricultural populations presented problems aggravated by the peace settlement. Sometimes alien national minorities appeared to threaten the state. Liberal institutions were only superficially implanted in many of the new countries and traditional conservative social and religious forces were strong. As in Latin America, where similar economic conditions could be found, their apparent constitutionalism tended to give way sooner or later to the rule of strong men and soldiers. This proved the case before 1939 in the new Baltic states, Poland and all the successor states of the Dual Monarchy except

General Miguel Primo de Rivera (1870–1930) led a military *coup d'état* in Spain in 1923, supported by the king and the army. He acted as the country's dictator until 1930, when the loss of the army's support forced him to resign.

Czechoslovakia, the one effective democracy in Central Europe or the Balkans. The need of these states to fall back on such régimes demonstrated both the unreality of the hopes entertained of their political maturity in 1918 and the new fear of Marxist communism, especially acute on Russia's borders. Such pressure operated also – though less acutely – in Spain and Portugal, where the influence of traditional conservatism was even stronger and Catholic social thinking counted for more than Fascism.

ECONOMIC RECOVERY

The failures of democracy between the wars did not proceed at an even pace; in the 1920s a bad economic start was followed by a gradual recovery of prosperity in which most of Europe outside Russia shared, and the years from 1925 to 1929 were on the whole good ones. This permitted optimism about the

General Carmona, president of the Portuguese republic from 1928 to 1951, is greeted by enthusiastic crowds in 1941. Next to him is Antonio de Oliveira Salazar, prime minister and the real dictator of Portugal from 1932 to 1968.

political future of the new democratic nations. Currencies emerged from appalling inflation in the first half of the decade and were once more stable; the resumption by many countries of the gold standard was a sign of confidence that the old pre-1914 days were returned. In 1925 the production of food and raw materials in Europe for the first time passed the 1913 figure and a recovery of manufacturing was also under way. With the help of a worldwide recovery of trade and huge investment from the United States, now an exporter of capital, Europe reached in 1929 a level of trade not to be touched again until 1954.

GERMAN ECONOMIC WEAKNESS

Yet collapse followed the boom of the 1920s. Economic recovery had been built on insecure foundations. When faced with a sudden crisis, the new prosperity crumbled rapidly. There followed not merely a European but a world economic crisis which was the single most important event between two world wars.

The complex but remarkably efficient economic system of 1914 had in fact been irreparably damaged. International exchange was hampered by a huge increase of restrictions immediately after the war as new nations strove to protect their infant economies with tariffs and exchange control, and bigger and older nations tried to repair their enfeebled ones. The Versailles treaty made things worse by saddling Germany, the most important of all the European industrial states, with an indefinite burden of reparation in kind and in cash. This not only distorted her economy and delayed its recovery for years, but also took away much of the incentive to make it work. To the east, Germany's greatest potential market, Russia, was almost

A French soldier accompanies a cargo of German coke to France as part of the reparations Germany was ordered to make to her former enemy at the end of the First World War.

entirely cut off behind an economic frontier which little trade could penetrate; the Danube valley and the Balkans, another great area of German enterprise, was divided and impoverished. Temporarily, these difficulties were gradually overcome by the availability of American money, which Americans were willing to supply (though they would not take European goods and retired behind their tariff walls). But this brought about a dangerous dependence on the continued prosperity of the United States.

AMERICAN BOOM AND SLUMP

In the 1920s the United States produced nearly 40 per cent of the world's coal and over half the world's manufactures. This abundance, enhanced by the demands of war, had transformed the life of many Americans, the first people in the world to be able to take for granted the possession of family automobiles. Unfortunately, American domestic prosperity carried the world. On it depended the confidence which provided American capital for export. Because of this, a swing in the business cycle turned into a world economic disaster. In 1928 short-term money began to be harder to get in the United States. There were also signs that the end of the long boom might be approaching. These two factors led to the calling back of American loans from Europe. Soon some European borrowers were in difficulties. Meanwhile, demand was slackening in the United States as people began to think a severe slump might be on the way. Almost accidentally, this detonated a particularly sudden and spectacular stock market collapse in October 1929. It did not matter that there was thereafter a temporary rally and that great bankers bought to restore confidence. It was the end of American business confidence and of over-

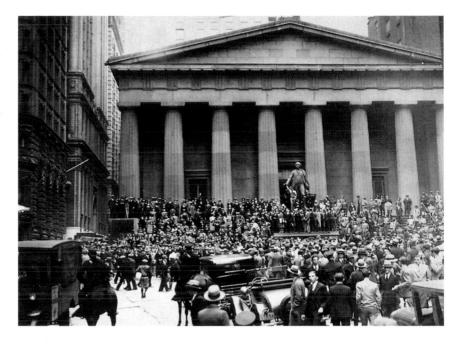

seas investment. After a last brief rally in 1930 American money for investment abroad dried up. The world slump began.

THE WORLD ECONOMY COLLAPSES

Economic growth came to an end because of the collapse of investment, but another factor was soon operating to accelerate disaster. As the debtor nations tried to put their accounts in order, they cut imports. This caused a drop in world prices, so that countries producing primary goods could not afford to buy abroad. Meanwhile, at the centre of things, both the United States and Europe went into a financial crisis; as countries struggled, unsuccessfully, to keep the value of their currencies steady in relation to gold (an internationally acceptable means of exchange – hence the expression "gold standard") they adopted deflationary policies to balance their books which again cut demand. By 1933 all the major currencies, except the French, were off gold. This was the symbolic expression of the tragedy, the dethronement of one old idol

Horrified crowds gather in front of the Treasury Building on New York's Wall Street in 1929 as news of the stock market crash breaks.

An American soup kitchen distributes free food to the poor during the Depression.

and the poorer sectors of the mature economies suffered disproportionately. They may not always have seemed to do so, because they had less far to fall; an Eastern European or an Argentinian peasant may not have been absolutely much worse off for he was always badly off, while an unemployed German clerk or factory hand certainly was worse off and knew it.

THE DECAY OF EUROPEAN HEGEMONY

There was to be no world recovery before another great war. Nations cut themselves off more and more behind tariffs and strove in some cases to achieve economic self-sufficiency by an increasing state control of their economic life. Some did better than others, some very badly. The disaster was a promising setting for the Communists and Fascists who expected or advocated the collapse of liberal civilization and now began to flap expectantly about the enfeebled carcass. The end of the gold standard and the belief in non-interference with the economy mark the collapse of a world order in its economic dimension as strikingly as the rise of totalitarian régimes and the rise of nationalism to its destructive climax mark it in its political. Liberal civilization, frighteningly, had lost its power to control events. Many Europeans still found it hard to see this, though, and they continued to dream of the restoration of an age when that civilization enjoyed unquestioned supremacy. They forgot that its values had rested on a political and economic hegemony which, for a time, had worked but was already visibly in decay all round the world.

of liberal economics. Its reality was a level of unemployment which may have reached thirty million in the industrial world. In 1932 (the worst year for industrial countries) the index of industrial production for the United States and Germany was in each case only just above half of what it had been in 1929.

The effects of economic depression rolled outwards with a ghastly and irresistible logic. The social gains of the 1920s, when many people's standard of living had improved, were wiped out. No country had a solution to unemployment and though it was at its worst in the United States and Germany it existed in a concealed form all round the world in the villages and farmlands of the primary producers. The national income of the United States fell by 38 per cent between 1929 and 1932; this was exactly the figure by which the prices of manufactured goods fell, but at the same time raw material prices fell by 56 per cent and foodstuffs by 48 per cent respectively. Everywhere, therefore, the poorer nations

New York's Broadway is pictured in 1928 – the year before the bubble burst. The carefree 1920s, when America and Europe enjoyed a period of relative prosperity, were almost over. Such untroubled times would soon become a distant memory, as the world prepared to enter another devastating global war.

Time chart (1800–1925)

1807
Britain abolishes
the slave trade

1810–1822
Emancipation of
Latin America

1805

1810

The French began their conquest of
Algeria in 1830 and completed it in
1839. This scene from that period is
entitled *Arab Chiefs Meeting in
Council* and was painted in 1834.

Arab chiefs in Algeria

First steam-
propelled railway

1827
Ohm's law of
electric conductance

1825

1830

1831
Faraday's law of
electromagnetic induction

1846
Morton invents
anaesthetic

1847
Hoe invents the
rotary printing press

1848
Revolutions
in Europe

1850–1864
Taiping insurrection
in China

1845

1850

The first ship sails through the Suez
Canal in Egypt on its opening day,
17 November, 1869. The completion of
the canal drastically shortened the
journey between Europe and Asia.

Suez Canal

1864
First Socialist
International

1867
Creation of Dual Monarchy
of Austria-Hungary

1865

1870

1868
The Meiji Restoration
in Japan

1870–1871
Franco-Prussian War

1871
German Unification

The French painter Paul Gauguin
(1848–1903) settled in Tahiti in
1891 and depicted the island
women in canvases such
as this one.

Tahitian Women at the Beach

1884–1885
Berlin Conference
on Africa

The Indian National
Congress is founded

1889
Second Socialist
International

1885

1890

1893
Women obtain the
vote in New Zealand

Ceramic figure

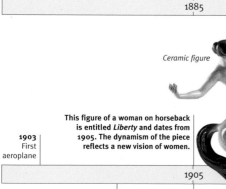

This figure of a woman on horseback
is entitled *Liberty* and dates from
1905. The dynamism of the piece
reflects a new vision of women.

1903
First
aeroplane

1905

1910

1904–1905
Russo-
Japanese War

1905
Einstein's special
theory of relativity

1911–1912
Republican revolution
in China

1816
Argentina declares
independence

1818
India becomes a
British dominion

1815

Treaty of Vienna

1820

Following his victories against the
Spanish, the independence movement
leader Simón Bolívar (1783–1830) was
declared president of the Republic of
Colombia in 1819.

Simón Bolívar

1834
Slavery is abolished
in the British colonies

1839–1842
First Opium War

1842
China is opened
to the West

1835

1840

1839
Photography invented

Charles Darwin (1809–1882)
revolutionized concepts about living
beings with his theory of evolution,
which he outlined in *The Origin of
Species*, first published in 1859.

Charles Darwin

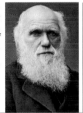

1853–1856
The Crimean War

1861
The Unification of Italy

1855

1860

1861–1865
The American Civil War

1876
Queen Victoria is
crowned Empress
of India

1878
Edison invents the
incandescent
electric lamp

1882
Koch discovers the bacterium
responsible for tuberculosis

1875

1880

In 1894 Sun Yat-sen founded the
**Association for the Regeneration of
China**, a revolutionary movement calling
for national independence, agrarian
reform and the formation of a republic.

Sun Yat-sen

1896
Marconi invents
radio-telegraphy

From 1899 to 1900 combined
international Western forces
attempted to combat the
xenophobic Boxer movement in
China. Here, German sailors are
depicted fighting the Boxers.

Chinese Boxer movement

1895

1900

1894–1895
Sino-Japanese War

Lumière brothers
invent cinematograph

1899–1902
The Boer War

Planck formulates
the quantum theory

A Mk V tank goes into action during
the First World War. The war lasted
from 1914 until 1918 and caused
destruction and loss of life in
Europe on an unprecedented scale.

First World War tank

The League of
Nations is founded

1922
Triumph of
Fascism in Italy

1915

1920

1917
The Russian Revolution

VOLUME 8 *Chapters and contents*

Chapter 4

Strains in the system 106

Chapter 5

The era of the First World War 134

SERIES CONTENTS

INDEX

Page references to main text in roman, to box text in **bold** and to captions in *italic*.

ACKNOWLEDGMENTS

The publishers wish to thank the following for their kind permission to reproduce the illustrations in this book:

KEY
b below; **c** centre; **t** top; **l** left; **r** right
AGE: AGE Fotostock
AISA: Archivo Iconografico S.A.
AKG: AKG London
BAL: Bridgeman Art Library, London / New York
BL: British Library, London
BN: Bibliothèque Nationale, Paris
ET: e.t. Archive, London
IWM: Imperial War Museum, London
JLC: Jean-Loup Charmet, Paris
V&A: By courtesy of the board of trustees of the Victoria & Albert Museum, London

Front Cover: BL / Oriental and India Office Collections
3 BAL / Novosti
7 BL / Oriental & India Office Collections. Mss Eurf.111/270 No.35
8 Hulton Getty
10 AKG
11 AISA
12 AISA
13 AISA
14 AISA
15t AGE
15b AISA
16 AGE
17t AISA / Bibliothèque des Arts Décoratifs, Paris
17b AISA
18 Popperfoto
19 Zardoya / Camera Press Ltd, London
20 Hulton Getty
21 AISA
22 AISA
23 AISA
24 AISA / Museo Nacional de Historia, Mexico
25 AISA
26 AISA / Museo Municipal, Quito
27 AISA
28 AISA
29t AISA / Biblioteca de Ajuda, Lisbon
29b AISA
30 BAL / Private Collection
31 Punch Library, London
32 AISA
33 AISA
34 AISA
35 AISA
36 AISA
37 AGE
38 AGE
39 AGE
41 JLC

42 AISA
43 AISA
44 Zardoya / Camera Press Ltd, London / Bassano
45t AISA / Bibliothèque des Arts Décoratifs, Paris
45b AISA
46 AGE
47 AISA
48 AISA / V&A
49 Hulton Getty
50 AISA / BN
52 AISA / Musée Condé, Chantilly
53 AISA
57 AISA
58 AISA
59 AISA / Musée des Beaux-Arts, Orléans
60 AISA / Musée d'Orsay, Paris
61 AISA
62 AISA
63 Popperfoto
65 Hulton Getty
66 AISA / BN
67 AGE
68 AGE
69 AGE
72 ET / Private Collection
73 AISA
74 AISA
75 AISA
76 AISA
77t AISA
77b Zardoya
78 Popperfoto
79 AISA / Museo d'Arte Orientale "Edoardo Chiossonè", Genova
80 AISA / Museo d'Arte Orientale "Edoardo Chiossonè", Genova
81 AGE
82 AISA
84 AISA
85 Kyodo News, Tokyo
87 AISA
88 AISA
89 AISA / Galerie de l'Imagerie, Paris
90 AISA
92 AISA / V&A
93 AISA
94 AISA
96 BL / Oriental & India Office Collections
98 AISA
100 AISA
101 AISA
102 Roger-Viollet
104 Roger-Viollet
105 Roger-Viollet / Branger
106 Zardoya / Camera Press Ltd, London
108 AISA / Musée d'Orsay, Paris
110t Zardoya / Camera Press Ltd, London
110b AISA
111 AISA
112 BAL / Giraudon / Bibliothèque de l'Assemblée Nationale, Paris

113 Roger-Viollet / Cap
114 AISA / BN
115 AISA
116 AISA
117 Popperfoto
118 AISA
119 AISA
120 AGE
121 Zardoya / Camera Press Ltd, London
122 AISA
123 AISA
125 Popperfoto
126 AISA / Biblioteca Nacional, Madrid
128 AISA
129 AGE / Science Photo Library / JLC
130 AGE
133 Punch Library, London
134 AISA
135 AISA / Musée National du Château de Versailles, Paris
136 ET
137 Popperfoto
138 Hulton Getty
139 ET / IWM
140 ET
141 AGE
142 JLC
143 AISA
144 Hulton Getty
145 Zardoya / Camera Press Ltd, London
147t AGE
147b AGE
148 Zardoya / Camera Press Ltd, London / IWM
149 ET
150 AGE
151 Zardoya / Camera Press Ltd, London / IWM
152 AGE
153 BAL / Novosti
154t Zardoya / Camera Press Ltd, London
154b AISA
155 AISA
157 ET / Syndication International (Daily Mirror), London
158t Archive Photos / Image Bank
158b AISA
159 ET / IWM
160 AISA
161 Popperfoto
162 Hulton Getty
163 AISA
164 AGE
167 Roger-Viollet / Harlingue
168 AISA / State Tretyakov Gallery, Moscow
169 Zardoya / Camera Press Ltd, London
170 AGE
171 AISA
172 Roger-Viollet
173 Zardoya / Camera Press Ltd, London
174t AGE
174b Popperfoto
175 AISA
176 Hulton Getty

177 Archive Photos / Image Bank
178 AGE
179 AGE

MAPS
All maps copyright © 1998 Helicon/Debate

TEXT CREDITS
The publishers wish to thank the following for their kind permission to reproduce the translations and copyright material in this book. Every effort has been made to trace copyright owners, but if anyone has been omitted we apologize and will, if informed, make corrections in any future edition.

p.54 extract from *The White Man's Burden* by Rudyard Kipling (Kyle Cathie 1990). Reproduced by permission of A. P. Watt Ltd. on behalf of The National Trust for Places of Historic Interest or Natural Beauty; p.166 extract from *'Left Wing' Communism: an infantile disorder* by Vladimir Ilyich Lenin (Bookmarks 1993). Reproduced by permission of Bookmarks.